▲ Shivpuri

£2.49

Vajrajogini

Gokarna

GOKARNA BAN FOREST

Sankhu

Changunarayan

Nagarkot

R.

Bode

Nakades

Thimi

e R.

Bhaktapur

Nala

Sanga

Banepa

Godaveri Botanical Garden

Panauti

▲ Phulchowki

0   4 km

Kathmandu Valley

This metal trident—a symbol of the god Shiva—stands on top of Phulchowki hill, at the southern edge of Kathmandu Valley. Kathmandu City lies to the northwest.

THIS BEAUTIFUL WORLD   VOL. 61

Kathmandu Valley

ROBERT L. FLEMING, JR.

LINDA F. FLEMING

 KODANSHA INTERNATIONAL LTD.
TOKYO, NEW YORK & SAN FRANCISCO

Distributors:

UNITED STATES: *Kodansha International/USA, Ltd., through Harper & Row, Publishers, Inc., 10 East 53rd Street, New York, New York 10022.* SOUTH AMERICA: *Harper & Row, Publishers, Inc., International Department.* CANADA: *Fitzhenry & Whiteside Ltd., 150 Lesmill Road, Don Mills, Ontario M3B 2T6.* MEXICO AND CENTRAL AMERICA: *HARLA S. A. de C. V., Apartado 30–546, Mexico 4, D. F.* UNITED KINGDOM: *Phaidon Press Ltd., Littlegate House, St. Ebbe's Street, Oxford OX1 1SQ.* EUROPE: *Boxerbooks Inc., Limmatstrasse 111, 8031 Zurich.* AUSTRALIA AND NEW ZEALAND: *Book Wise (Australia) Pty. Ltd., 104–8 Sussex Street, Sydney 2000.* THE FAR EAST: *Toppan Company (S) Pte. Ltd., No. 38, Liu Fang Road, Jurong, Singapore 22.*

Published by Kodansha International Ltd., 2–12–21 Otowa, Bunkyo-ku, Tokyo 112 and Kodansha International/USA, Ltd., 10 East 53rd Street, New York, New York 10022 and 44 Montgomery Street, San Francisco, California 94104. Copyright in Japan 1978 by Kodansha International Ltd. All rights reserved. Printed in Japan.

LCC 77–15371
ISBN 0–87011–328–3
JBC 0326–786229–2361

First edition, 1978

Contents

Contents

Drawings by Hirobumi Nagakane

Swayambhu
A Burning Lotus

"Green, so vibrantly green," remarks our elderly guest as we pass rice fields brilliantly backlit by the late afternoon sun. We are driving toward Swayambhu Stupa at the western edge of Kathmandu Valley. "I've never seen anything like it."

The rain-washed summer air at 4,500 feet (1372 meters) accents each color with additional sparkle, the rich tones saturated more deeply than those encountered in hazy or dust-filled urban surroundings.

Yes, she probably hasn't seen anything like Kathmandu, for there *is* no other place like Kathmandu—not in Nepal, not in the Himalayas, not in all Asia.

Leaving our taxi at the parking shelf halfway up the hill, we puff onward, climbing past gaudily painted images of Buddhas, white chaityas and spreading, subtropical trees. Brown rhesus monkeys, squabbling and chattering, dash across the path in front. Finally, some two hundred feet above the Valley floor, we emerge onto a level stone platform dominated by the main Swayambhu Stupa, its white dome and gilded tower surrounded by numerous shrines, idols, curio shops and an active monastery, the entire area bustling with local people, other tourists, monkeys, dogs and goats. Swayambhu, with its swirling activity, encapsulates a seemingly chaotic yet wonderfully operative blend of

7

Asian cultures, traditions and peoples. Here Asian east meets Asian west, the total augmented by influences from the north and many from the south.

Swayambhu is a splendid place to begin a visit to Kathmandu, for from here one can see the bowllike configuration of the Valley, its almost 204-square-mile floor enclosed on all sides by hills. Through this fertile scene wind the shimmering lines of the sacred Vishnumati and Bagmati rivers, and behind, far to the north, white peaks rise silhouetted, improbable and almost unreal, against the sky. Formerly a lake bed, the Valley now stands as a testimony to the ingenuity and industriousness—and comparative gentleness—of the Nepalese people. Every inch seems used: fields neatly terraced, rural villages guarding ripening crops, dark green forest groves shading sacred shrines between noisy and congested urban centers. With over two thousand holy spots dotting the Valley, the poetic name *devbhumi* ("home of the gods") is aptly taken.

Not that Kathmandu has always been peaceful or entirely hospitable to religion and the arts. Intrigue, plenty of it, filled some years with slaughters and mini-wars. But today Kathmandu has emerged largely unscathed and, in places, virtually unchanged from centuries of isolation.

Isolated Nepal has certainly been. Its mountain terrain saw to that, separating Kathmandu from the great plains of India. But one cannot help feeling that the people deliberately bolstered the barriers. Thus the early Chinese scholar, Hsuan-tsang, writing of the Nepalese in about A.D. 650, said: "The inhabitants are all of a hard and savage nature. . . ." Knowing the Nepalese today, one can imagine those early residents cultivating this harsh reputation to discourage outside depredation in their remote country.

Swayambhu hill features prominently in the mythical origins of the Valley; to start one's visit here has symbolic significance.

Many an evening tale is told of how Kathmandu came to be, and one of the most picturesque versions follows. Once upon a time, Kathmandu Valley was surrounded by forests and filled with deep, clear water wherein dwelt numerous gods and a pantheon of snake deities. In those early days, Kathmandu was called Naghrad, "the abode of snakes." Naturally the lake, considered very holy, was visited by many pilgrims, who came from the far corners of the earth. Buddhas and Boddhisatvas (demigods dedicated to helping man) came and went, communing with the deities and admiring the lake with its many lotus plants. One day, quite suddenly and spontaneously, a certain lotus growing well out in the water spouted a brilliant flame. But even without such fire, this was no ordinary flower, for it shone with gold and precious stones. The pistils of the flower, for example, reflected the blue of lapis lazuli. And the flame, which burned brighter even than the sun, was recognized as the miraculous manifestation of Adi-Buddha, or the Godhead.

It seems, the legend continues, that on one occasion Manjushri (a Boddhisatva who lived in remote Manchuria, northern China) decided to journey to Nag-hrad to worship the Godhead. Upon arrival, he thrice circumambulated the lake and thereupon decided that on this holy ground his followers would settle; here they should build shrines and pray, here they would dwell in peace. So Manjushri drew his sword (Vishnu plays this role in the Hindu version) and smote the retaining hill, releasing the waters of the lake which, gushing fiercely through the gorge (now called Chobar, or "sword cut"), carried with them various snakes and assorted monsters. Only the King of the Snakes, the Karkotak Nag, was allowed by Manjushri to remain behind to control the eventual wealth of the new valley. (As we shall see, Nag still lives near Chobar—under Taudha Pond, to be exact—and features prominently in one of the biggest festivals of the year.) And as the clear waters receded, the sacred lotus, still aflame, metamorphosed into what is now Swayambhu hill.

Today a large stupa glitters on Swayambhu. A stupa, by definition, is a domed structure and houses a relic of some saint, while a chaitya (we passed several on the way up the hill) is of similar shape but contains no relics. As we admire Swayambhu Stupa, we draw our friend's attention to details in the scene around us and show her the 211 prayer wheels that encircle the white dome at shoulder height. These Tibetan Buddhist instruments hold the sacred mantra *om mani padme hum* and other prayers that become activated with a clockwise motion (with each revolution, prayers are stored in heaven on the supplicant's behalf).

Above the prayer wheels and the white dome rises a gilded tower. This metal-plated structure, square at the base, displays four pairs of eyes (one pair for each compass point), painted in orange, white, blue and black. Between each set of eyes, in the position of a nose, is a figure resembling a question mark, which represents the Vedic symbol for the number "1"—the figure signifying Buddha's primacy among the gods, and the eyes his eternal watchfulness over his followers. This facial base is crowned with thirteen graduated metal disks or "umbrellas," representing the stages to heaven. The main Swayambhu superstructure claims rather recent origin, but the site has traditionally been held sacred for over twenty centuries.

Immediately north of the stupa perches a modern three-story monastery complex run by Tibetan Karma-pa (Red Hat) monks, whose abbot, a personable Tibetan of late middle age, is an avatar or *rimpoche*, a reincarnation of a former pious lama. Punctuated by the sound of drums, cymbals and horns, the voices of praying monks can be heard each afternoon in a ground-floor room behind a gleaming statue of Buddha (ten feet high, the largest in Kathmandu).

Directly west of the main stupa, its upturned eaves hardly thirty feet from the white dome, stands a richly ornamented temple dedicated to the Sitala Ajima, the Hindu Goddess of Smallpox. Each day numerous devotees bring flowers, rice and colored powders to the temple, insuring themselves against future illnesses of all varieties. Incense, competing with the smoke from oil lamps, hovers about the silver idol.

Buddhism intermingles with Hinduism at Swayambhu—as it does throughout the Valley. Temples and monasteries side by side, Buddha shrines and Shiva lingams often only inches apart, all speak of a wonderful religious tolerance traditional in Kathmandu through the centuries. No iconoclasm has defaced the rich religious art of the sequestered Valley. No great forts stand as crumbling relics of a warlike past. This is a peaceful region where people of differing backgrounds make a point of getting along. The question, "Are you a Buddhist or a Hindu?" is often greeted in Kathmandu by: "Why, we don't distinguish, we worship at all shrines. Sometimes Hindu, sometimes Buddhist." An amazing attitude when one thinks of the religious divisions that exist elsewhere in today's world.

Thus the sensations that press upon one at Swayambhu, the noise, the bustle, the smells, the tolerant attitude of man toward his fellow animals, the colorful glimpses of monuments and powder-sprinkled idols, are, in a nutshell, the essence and uniqueness that is Kathmandu Valley.

Our friend, after viewing the Valley's broad expanse and rubbing shoulders with lamas and monkeys while inhaling smoke from incense sticks and butter lamps, indicates she wishes to return to her hotel. On descending to our yellow-roofed Toyota taxi, we glide down the hill, first passing Ananda Kuti Vidyapeet, an all-boys Buddhist private school with a high reputation in Kathmandu's educational circles. Then, on the right, comes the

Natural History Museum, which houses collections (especially birds and butterflies) of Nepal's rich fauna and flora.

At the bottom of the hill we pass the New Tibetan Yak Restaurant, with several long-haired, rather unkempt Westerners lounging nearby. This lower part of Swayambhu used to be the Mecca of the "hippie subculture" that developed rapidly—and with much publicity—in Kathmandu some years ago. There was a time when one could count on seeing dozens of foreigners in various modes of dress relaxing around the base of Swayambhu, but the bloom is now off. "BEST JUMLA HASHISH SOLD HERE" the signs used to read, and Cannabis Cookies were once a favorite item in "Freak Street" hotels. Little remains of the earlier era. Apparently few Nepalese were happy with the mushrooming publicity their open-door policy garnered or with the effect these people had on the youth of the Valley. Suddenly, and without warning, the government cracked down, banning overnight the sale of marijuana and making visa extensions more expensive and harder to obtain.

Easing onto the plain from Swayambhu hill, we skirt an army firing range and approach the National Museum complex, whose fine collection of weapons used in various historic Gurkha battles, and splendid bronze and stone images from Kathmandu's past, make a visit well worthwhile.

The taxi rattles under the porte cochere of the Malla Hotel, where we escort our guest into the lobby to bid her, temporarily, good-bye. This hotel is a fine example of a moderate-sized Nepali tourist accommodation striving to be both tasteful and comfortable. The lobby attractively highlights Nepali decor and motifs, with one part, for instance, featuring two large oil murals—impressions of Himalayan peaks done by Lain S. Bangdel, Nepal's leading artist. And the wood carvings here illustrate the work of master Newari craftsmen.

For the following day we have arranged for our guest to take a city tour operated by a local travel agency. Fortunately there are a number of reliable outfits in Kathmandu—useful services not only for visitors but also for local residents who can book guests on tours, thus freeing them from a stream of temple visits. We usually recommend that guests first take a fast-paced general tour to obtain an overall idea of the area, and then, when they decide where to spend more time, we take them back for a more leisurely visit.

Our guest calls the next evening to report that she has had a grand day and wishes to spend additional time poking about the old, downtown part of Kathmandu City. Her first glimpse of it proved fascinating; she is now tempted to see more, to feel the pulse of the city and absorb its history.

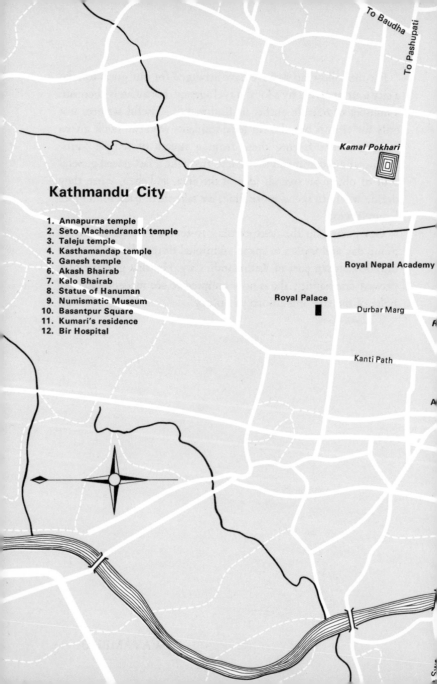

Kathmandu City

1. Annapurna temple
2. Seto Machendranath temple
3. Taleju temple
4. Kasthamandap temple
5. Ganesh temple
6. Akash Bhairab
7. Kalo Bhairab
8. Statue of Hanuman
9. Numismatic Museum
10. Basantpur Square
11. Kumari's residence
12. Bir Hospital

To Baudha

To Pashupati

Kamal Pokhari

Royal Nepal Academy

Royal Palace

Durbar Marg

Kanti Path

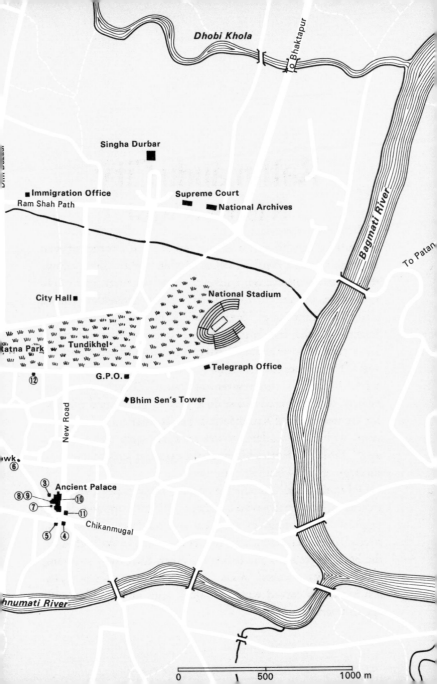

Dhobi Khola

To Bhaktapur

Singha Durbar

■ Immigration Office
Ram Shah Path

Supreme Court

National Archives

Bagmati River

To Patan

City Hall ■

National Stadium

Ratna Park

Tundikhel

⑫

G.P.O. ■

♦ Bhim Sen's Tower

Telegraph Office

New Road

wk
⑥

③ Ancient Palace
⑧⑨
⑦   ⑩
⑪
⑤ ④
Chikanmugal

hnumati River

0   500   1000 m

Kathmandu City
A Temple of Wood

We call for her the next morning and drive to a corner of Rani Pokhari, Queen's Pond, in which a whitewashed Shiva temple stands; here we leave our conveyance and penetrate, past a "No Cars" sign, into the crowded old city, via a thoroughfare known casually as "Bike Street," for it is flanked by bicycle rental stores. Various vehicles, mostly painted black and showing considerable wear, roost in rows along the street (no sidewalks here). And the cost? "Five rupees (US$0.42) a day," answers a dealer. And for a week? "Why, five times seven, of course." Bicycles are a convenient though slightly hazardous way to get around the city, for the main part of Kathmandu is hardly three miles long by as many wide; even outlying towns are never more than ten miles away. From the battered look of the cycles, it seems there is no shortage of hard-pedaling customers.

Old Kathmandu was built for people—not vehicles. Even cycle rickshaws, their rubber-bulbed horns stridently tooting, barely negotiate the throngs of shoppers and residents. The narrow streets have venerable Newari houses crowding in on both sides, the buildings stacked one beside the other, their roofs sweeping continuously for several "houses" together. Many residences possess intricately carved window frames, some now splitting with age and decay.

As we enter Asan Tol—one of the busiest and most tightly packed markets in Kathmandu, or in the entire Himalayas for that matter—we find an open square. Well, not exactly open, for scores of people bargaining, selling, or just spectating clog the space. Bags of rice, shadowed by the three-story Annapurna temple, decorate the southeast edge of Asan. On the grain in each bag rests an iron mug (one *mana* in volume), waiting to be heaped for another sale. Buyers expertly finger, smell, and even taste the grain before completing transactions; for rice is important in Kathmandu—a fact quickly confirmed by a visit to Asan when merchant and customer are in full cry. Indeed, anyone with an ear for market opera would be excited by Asan at busy moments, though all the voices in the ensemble might be hard to identify, for Nepali, Newari, Tamang and Tibetan mingle with a dozen other languages in the square. And to this babel of tongues are joined the ringing of bells, the quarreling of dogs, the chanting of prayers, the advertising of herbal medicines, the half-crow of a young, caged cock, the challenge of a meandering bull and, above it all, the twittering of swallows and swifts as they dart to nests beneath the eaves of Asan houses.

Color swirls past: red saris, pink and lavender ones too, with big flower prints, bright blue shirts above purple trousers, gaily painted rickshaws and a saffron-robed priest—all hurry by in a bright montage. Stores display color-saturated cloth, pink plastic sandals and multihued nylon ropes. Small splashes of color draw attention to scented flowers in a girl's hair, a vermilion spot on a cow's forehead, a red-powdered idol of Ganesh, and well-scrubbed carrots tiered for display in wicker baskets.

To some, Asan is an almost overwhelming experience. All one's senses and instincts are involved—including that of survival. Young cyclists dash through the crowd while not-to-be-denied cows shove toward cauliflower greens. Pushcarts pose an additional hazard. These contraptions, made of flat boards arranged above pneumatic rubber tires, are guided from behind by muscular men straining to see (often unsuccessfully) where they are going—their vision partly blocked by high piles of sundry merchandise ranging from filing cabinets to red-upholstered furniture or jute gunnysacks lumpy with onions.

Small streets lined with busy shops radiate from Asan. Stores smelling of wax display candles varying from fat and short to thin and long; some are red, others blue, pink and orange (white, the color of mourning, is not common). These candles light easily, but sputter and fume as the wax burns faster than the wick, soon leaving the latter a long and smoking stalk. Other enterprises here sell dry goods, ropes, baskets, paints and umbrellas.

As we move southwest from Asan, treading deeper into old Kathmandu, people continue to teem, literally streaming past —colorful, talkative, active. Low shops, often framed in carved wood, front the street. Shopkeepers, mostly Newari, sit cross-legged in pockets of space, hemmed in by the goods overflowing their counters. Specialty stores feature hardware items from nails to chicken wire, while cloth merchants supply local cottons and imported polyesters. The Grand Wool Center competes with warm, ready-made garments, and the Siska Optical Company displays a fairly conventional range of glasses. One may also bargain for brass vessels, plastic boxes and aluminum pans amid the hubbub.

The pans store advertises its supply with a six-foot-high pyramid of aluminum pans jammed just outside the wooden door. A good thing they are outside; certainly no room appears inside. Squeezed into a space hardly eleven feet wide, eight feet deep, and five and a half feet high are dozens of brass, aluminum, enamel and plastic pots, pans, pitchers, pressure cookers, stoves, plates, cups, telescoping lunch carriers, numerous smaller items—and one merchant. This salesman serves several customers at once while they lean into the doorway straining to see the goods. Sales move slowly as aluminum objects sell according to weight. None are pre-marked, so each must be weighed on a pair of scales, the merchant adding or removing iron weights to make the two sides balance.

The Nepal Cap House adjoins the pans store. The owner, also cross-legged on the floor, is always busy—Nepali men need caps. In fact, the Nepali cap, a tightly worn, brimless object not unlike a fez, is one of the symbols of Nepal, and all officials must wear the cap in government offices. While the formal cap is black and stiff, the casual ones sport many colors and fairly elaborate designs. The origin of the cap is obscure, but a popular version suggests it resembles the shape of a Himalayan peak—as good an explanation as any other, perhaps.

On the right, and slightly beyond the Cap House, stands a tall flower-carved stone pillar crowned by back-to-back Buddhas. Behind this decorative object, a low passageway leads to an inner courtyard crowded with figures (including seven lotus-pedestaled images on pillars that stand well over six feet high) and dominated at the center by a magnificent temple. This Seto Machendranath temple, dedicated to the Boddhisatva Arya-lokiteshvara, stands hidden from the main street, illustrating the compactness and complexity of downtown Kathmandu. Here, a major temple can rest unseen from thirty yards away. Each spring, in March or April (depending on the moon), the silver image of the Seto Machendranath is paraded with great festivity through the streets of Kathmandu, and is returned to the temple on the night of the full moon.

While admiring the unusual hanging brass plates, we pass the main structure to duck through another passage (on the far side of the courtyard) and emerge into a maze of pots. Clay pots.

This is the pottery sales center of Kathmandu. Merchandise seems to flow from the open doors of houses abutting on the Machendranath courtyard. Pots and containers of all sizes and shapes. Vases, some molded in the form of elephants standing a foot high, are popular. Huge round pots may be used to hold grain, medium ones for water, and small varieties to store ashes from funeral pyres. Other creations serve as cups for tea, plates for oil lamps, dishes for yogurt, and holders for the coals of hubble-bubble pipes. Reddish items abound, spreading up the plinths of a temple opposite, but all must be arranged and moved with care for they are only bisque-fired (experimental glazing has just begun at the government cottage-industries center).

The space here is not completely devoted to pottery, for a covey of barbers flash straight razors and sharpened scissors on the lowest plinth. Rates stay extremely low: a complete shave—face *and* head—for five rupees (US$0.42) and a simple haircut for two rupees (US$0.16). The cut hair, black and usually short, is carefully gathered to be delivered, on a yearly contract basis, for use in making *mull*, or fertilizer. "Makes the plants grow exceptionally well," one barber explained. How he knew we were not sure.

Working back to the main street and again heading southwest—toward the royal center of ancient Kathmandu—we come to yet another grouping of temples around a bustling intersection. These temples stand upon three-tiered plinths of stone, most of which are draped with homemade rugs and shawls. Most Nepalese rugs, loosely woven of wool, rely on the natural colors of the wool; the result is gray backgrounds with dark (usually brown) designs. They are attractive and inexpensive.

From this three-tiered "rug stand" we survey Indra Chowk, an open square named for the Rain God, Indra. A busy temple dedicated to the Sky God (Akash Bhairab) fills the western side of the square. The Bhairab image, unusually placed at the second-story level, can be reached by a narrow staircase; every evening people gather around the idol to chant prayers, their rapt faces illuminated by naked light bulbs and a fluorescent tube. Their voices are accompanied by *tabla* or *madal* drums and a harmonium (a small, bellows-operated hand organ with a pianolike keyboard reminiscent of an accordion).

The Indra Chowk intersection is always packed. Garland sellers drape their wares in golden profusion, each band diffusing an early morning glow. Bunches of bananas hang over piles of apples and mangoes in street-side fruit stalls. Dogs nap in groups at the foot of a gilded lion, passersby taking care not to tread on recumbent forms.

Southwest of Indra Chowk the way narrows, and the eaves of eastern houses, separated by only six yards from opposing buildings, overhang the road. This is "Cloth Row," with stall after stall offering bright Indian and Chinese fabrics. So many stores crowd in upon each other that one fails to understand how they survive competition as none advertises and each seems to carry an equally colorful array.

At this point, rain clouds threaten, so we climb three steps into a convenient cloth store to wait out the shower. Sitting amid gaudy bolts of material, we review for our guest the seasons of Kathmandu. Rain is a feature of the June-to-September season, with showers almost every day. But in Kathmandu City, with only some sixty inches of rainfall a year, the precipitation is rarely prolonged or heavy. Clear weather reigns from November through May, with three or four unsettled periods in the winter or early spring. Snow was last seen on the Valley floor in 1944, but each winter it dusts down to 6,000 feet on the hills surrounding the Valley.

We watch people crouching under black umbrellas as they scurry past: raincoats are rare here, except on traffic police. Soon the rain-producing nimbus clouds shift west, so we thank the cloth-store man and step back onto the road, taking care not to slip on the glistening tarmac. Fifty yards farther southwest we reach another opening, this one paved with chiseled flagstones and brick. But we hardly glance at the stones, so eye-filling is the grand Taleju temple looming above an intervening row of shops. We have now arrived at the ancient heart of Kathmandu and will be hearing more of the name Taleju soon.

Maps designate this general area the Durbar (Palace) Square, but the locals usually speak of it as the Hanuman Dhoka area after the great statue of Hanuman, the Monkey God, who sits silently in stone atop a six-foot pedestal. Hanuman, arrayed in brilliant vermilion-orange paint, frequently receives sprinklings of flower petals from passing devotees. As this statue faces a temple with erotic carvings, Hanuman's eyes stay veiled, for the Monkey God, a symbol of disinterested goodwill, must be protected from temptation. Inserted into the brick wall near Hanuman is a fifteen-language stone inscription, dating from 1654, which features, among others, two words in French and one in English. Many were the influences felt in the Nepalese court in those days.

Near Hanuman we ascend a stairway that leads to a wide hall filled with cases of coins. This is Nepal's Numismatic Museum, and crossing the threshold to examine the coins—copper, silver and gold—is like stepping back into the history of Kathmandu.

The first recorded description of Nepal is by the famed Chinese scholar Hsuan-tsang who wrote in the seventh century that "the Kingdom of Ni-po-lo is some four thousand *li* in circumference [a *li* is about a third of a mile] and the capital is about twenty. It is situated in the midst of snowy mountains and itself constitutes an uninterrupted series of hills and valleys. Its soil is suited to the cultivation of grain, and abounds in flowers and fruits. One finds there red copper, yaks and birds of the name *ming ming*. Coins of red copper are used for exchange."

Indeed, these red coins are on display at the museum, showing that a Lichhavi king ruled during the time of Hsuan-tsang's writing. In fact, this Lichhavi dynasty, with interruptions from the Aviras, probably held sway during most of the early Christian era up to about the eighth century. It was the Lichhavi king Amashuvarma who, giving his daughter in marriage to the Tibetan king Srong-tsen-gam-po, introduced Buddhism into that country in A.D. 639 (the wedding date). And it was also during the Lichhavi period that a stone sculpture of Vishnu-Vikranta was carved. While this carving may not seem unusual, it was dated 388 Saka Sambat (equivalent to A.D. 467) and survives as the oldest known dated piece in Kathmandu, illustrating the fact that stone carving had reached a high standard in those early years.

Following the Lichhavis, the history of Nepal is confused— some five hundred years of confusion. Few coins, stone monuments, ancient manuscripts or even conflicting proclamations of who followed whom in dull royal genealogies have survived. This, it is thought, was the Thakuri period, when Kathmandu might have been a domain of the Gupta kings who held sway in the Ganges plain at that time. Moreover, it is held that, during this period, increased attention was paid to Tantric religious practices, probably strongly influenced by events in the Tantric centers of Bengal.

In any case, with the emergence of Ari Deva, the famous and well-documented Malla dynasty of Kathmandu began in the late twelfth century. Malla means "wrestler" in Sanskrit, and the story goes that the powerful Ari Deva was wrestling one afternoon when he was suddenly interrupted by an announcement that he had a son, an heir. "Name him Malla," the king declared.

Thus began a long line of Malla kings, men who patronized the arts and during whose rule wood carving, bronze casting and pagoda architecture flourished.

Many monuments now seen in Kathmandu date from the Malla period. This is true not only of structures but also of parks and forest preserves; Rani Ban Forest, walled and protected from encroachment in honor of a Malla queen in the 1600s, lies north of the Indian Embassy.

The founding father of Nepal as a modern nation was a dynamic warrior-king from Gurkha, a small principality sixty miles west of Kathmandu. In 1767 Prithvi Narayan Shah entered the Valley and after two years subdued the four Malla kingdoms that existed there. These four locations remain today in the cities of Kathmandu, Patan, Bhaktapur and Kirtipur, and the inner parts of the last two cities in particular have changed little since the days of the Gurkha conquerors.

Prithvi Narayan Shah, who minted numerous coins now on display at the Numismatic Museum, wished to control the Valley not only for the fertile fields it contained, but also because Kathmandu commanded the major trade routes from India to Tibet, thus earning great sums in taxes. The course of national consolidation begun by Prithvi Narayan ran through two generations, with his grandson, Rana Bahadur, extending the boundaries of Nepal to the Sutlej River in the west and through Sikkim in the east—with all activities directed from his throne in Kathmandu. Prithvi Narayan's great grandson, though, ran into the British; and when the treaty of Segauli was signed in 1816 and hostilities ceased, Nepal's boundaries were fixed between the rivers Mahakali and Mechi—where they remain today.

Following the establishment of Nepal's modern borders, only one generation of Shahs saw actual power in Kathmandu, for on September 15, 1846, Jung Bahadur Rana, a young nephew of the king, instigated the Kot massacre, eliminating in one evening over a hundred of the most prominent and powerful figures in Kathmandu. Thus began the Rana rule, a period of suppression and extreme isolation that lasted for 104 years.

Many reminders of the Rana past are scattered about Kathmandu Valley today. Bir Hospital dates from the time of Prime Minister Bir S.S.J.B. Rana (who ruled from 1881 to 1901), while Chandra S.S.J.B. Rana (r. 1901–1929) built the massive Singha Durbar Palace. (Chandra also introduced many exotic Australian trees such as the eucalyptus, bottle brush and silky oak.) Juddha S.S.J.B. Rana (r. 1932–1945) rebuilt part of Kathmandu after the great earthquake of 1934, and his statue stands at the west end of New Road. Moreover, many of the numerous palaces seen around town also date from this time—one palace for each of Juddha's acknowledged male offspring. Most of these palaces are used now not as residences but as large office buildings, and one (Shanta Bhawan) houses a mission hospital.

With the world changing rapidly outside the country, Nepal too began to feel the tide of change. The Shah kings, so long imprisoned in their palaces, stirred. Revolution became a possibility. Suddenly, one day in 1940, over a hundred men were arrested. "Traitors," claimed the prime minister. Five ringleaders were identified and charged, and four were promptly executed—two by hanging in public places and two shot (the fifth captive leader, a Brahmin and not subject to capital punishment, was imprisoned for life). Their crime? Secretly contacting the king. Today those four men are national heroes, their names learned by every schoolchild and their memory preserved in a modern structure on the Tundikhel (parade ground) called the "Martyrs' Arch." And indeed they were martyrs—dying for the developmental aspirations of the Nepalese.

In 1950, only ten years after the martyrs' demise, King Tribhuvan Shah, while driving to a picnic in the country, diverted suddenly (and unexpectedly, as far as the Rana prime minister was concerned) into the grounds of the Indian Embassy. The king quickly flew to India, triggering a revolution against the prime minister that had been brewing for some time. Faced with a popular uprising and forced to the wall, the prime minister agreed to changes in policy. King Tribhuvan returned to Nepal on February 15, 1951, to be greeted as the father of the new Nepal. Reforms immediately began, and within eighteen months the prime minister, Mohan S.S.J.B. Rana, retired to India.

Since 1951, "development" has been the cornerstone of royal policy, and Nepal—released from the shadow of Rana autocracy—made strides to catch up with the modern world. But the king, already weakened by a heart condition, died in 1955, at the age of forty-nine. Quickly taking over, Tribhuvan's son, Mahendra Bir Bikram Shah Dev, organized a democratic system of government in which many parties thrived—and bickered. Little was accomplished as ministry followed ministry, some only lasting a matter of days. Faced with the necessity of finding some cure for the nation's ills, King Mahendra, without warning, dismissed the parliament and took over the administration of the government himself, developing a "partyless panchayat" system rooted in the very culture of the Nepalese. "Panchayat" means a "meeting of five"—usually village elders and wise men who gathered to discuss village affairs—and from this tradition with deep historical roots the present nationwide system of panchayats has evolved.

Panchayat members are now elected to their positions. Several villages make up one panchayat, and from their midst the local panchayat members are elected, often after strenuous campaigning. These members select district-level representatives (there are seventy-five districts in Nepal) who, in turn, send delegates to the national panchayat which meets in Kathmandu. All legislation passes through this national body, which represents all the geographical regions of the country as well as the different strata of society. Of the 135 members of the national organization, 112 come from the various districts, and 23 are nominated by the king.

His Majesty King Birendra Bir Bikram Shah Dev, the grandson of Tribhuvan, ably rules today. The highly educated and well-traveled king places major emphasis on the economic development of his country; the fruits of this policy can be seen by any visitor to Kathmandu. Reorganization stands as a key idea in his administration: reorganization to increase efficiency and reduce waste. The educational system, for instance, has been remodeled from the primary-school roots up to the university level, and today one sees many students dressed in school uniforms hurrying to and from classes. Similarly, most government machinery, the Royal Nepal Academy, the National Sports Council—the list is endless—have responded to the voice of the king calling for more productivity, more efficiency, more selfless service to the nation. The king himself devotes all his energies to the development of the nation, and he urges his countrymen, many of whom revere him as an incarnation of Vishnu, to do the same.

Leaving the coin museum, we find Hanuman—still red and still blindfolded—perched on his stone pillar. Now we proceed east and, after paying a nominal fee, pass through an ornate door to the right of Hanuman to find ourselves in Nassal Chowk, a courtyard inside the ancient palace of Kathmandu. Our attention is first drawn to a black, stone-carved Narasimha graphically disemboweling an evil demon, while just beyond is a gallery with a prominent row of large black-framed portraits of the Shah dynasty, beginning with Prithvi Narayan and ending with the reigning monarch. Three stories above this gallery, on a pedestal protruding above the roof, is a gilded fish—a curious image, indeed, and thought by some to signify that directly below lies a large buried treasure left by the last Malla king.

Nassal Chowk is an important site as it is here that the kings of Nepal are crowned and that many traditional ceremonies involving the royal family are performed. On most days, however, the courtyard is relatively quiet, with guides and visitors occasionally crossing the chiseled flagstones, for the palace has become an architectural museum, preserving some of the finest wood carvings and buildings in the Valley. One can view the structure's inner layout by ascending a narrow and irregular staircase for nine floors, passing rooms empty except where one's imagination places potentates and courtiers of a long-gone era. Visitors persistent and careful enough to reach the top may gaze over Kathmandu's skyline, punctuated here and there by temple roofs or, more commonly, cement-coated buildings rising six or seven stories above street level.

Wood and brick do not survive endlessly in Kathmandu's climate. Ever since first admiring Kathmandu's great architectural treasures, art historians have urged that restoration proceed without delay. The government quickly agreed, and the Kathmandu Durbar was skillfully renovated between 1974 and 1977 under the auspices of UNESCO and the direction of John Sanday, a tall and affable Englishman trained in this art. Actually injecting the crumbling wood with a hardener is but one of many modern techniques used to restore old architectural masterpieces.

Clambering down from the tallest tower, we reach the flagged courtyard, pass the grisly Narasimha, and emerge into the street. Now, as we stand beside Hanuman, we can see, immediately to the right front, a fine pagoda with the familiar multistory roofs supported by wooden struts. These carved pieces, often garishly painted, feature figures of gods and goddesses. At the base of the struts one also finds, in some temples, small figures in erotic poses. Several explanations as to the significance of erotica in temple carvings circulate in Kathmandu; the most picturesque version, and very likely not the correct one, is that the Goddess of Lightning is a virgin and hence does not visit buildings with these displays. And in fact relatively few temples are struck, although they project far above the surrounding housetops. Some years ago, however, one in this very area was hit and damaged, and the inevitable bazaar talk had it that some goings-on in the temple had much displeased the goddess and drawn her wrath. Apparently things were rapidly corrected, for she has not been back.

Kathmandu's unique Newari temples can be distinguished instantly from pagoda forms in other Asian countries. In itself, the style of the Nepalese pagoda remains relatively static and unvarying. A temple will have from two to five roofs (only two temples have five tiers), graduated in size so that the smallest roof crowns the structure. The weight of the roofs is ingeniously distributed on pillars, struts and projecting brackets.

Iconographically, one of the most fascinating parts of these temples is the *torana*, an ornate panel placed above the entrance to the sanctuary of the idol. Made of wood or metal, the torana is strictly religious and usually depicts numerous deities or animals. The center of a common design features a leogryph, a mythological figure resembling a lion that grasps in its teeth two snakes which writhe around the torana, forming its border.

Another unique feature of a Nepalese temple, but not found on all structures, is a narrow band of gleaming metal (actually a series of plates carefully attached to one another) that usually cascades from the top pinnacle to below the rim of the lowest roof. These bands, or *pataka*, are not mere ornaments, but symbolize a pathway by which the deities can descend to humans who need their help. The lowest, or terminal, plate, also the largest in the series, may be cast with the highly decorated image of a god; others hang plain.

Small temple bells arrayed along the eaves of many temples have clappers attached to leaf-shaped paddles that catch the breeze; a Nepalese temple would look incomplete without these wind-bells delicately decorating the roofs, their chimes sounding man's devotion to his gods.

Kathmandu is a valley of bells. In the soft half-light of early morning, bells peel deeply in distant temple grounds, and soon nearby tinkling follows as neighbors rise to begin their daily *puja* (devotions). Large bells are rarely plain; most are elaborate affairs and some are intricately engraved, often with an inscription running along the outer rim. The Valley also boasts three giant bells—all hanging more than six feet long—and one of them is suspended directly before us as we stand near the Hanuman statue. This bell, cast for a Newari king over two centuries ago, was rung on special occasions and summoned people to religious events.

Thirty yards from the great bell (and forty from Hanuman) looms a fearsome black Kalo Bhairab figure with six arms and a necklace of twenty-one severed heads. Bhairab is the male consort of the goddess Durga, the Goddess of Destruction. Bhairab appears in many forms—sixty-four according to one reckoning—and is propitiated in different ways. If a man tells a falsehood in front of this Kalo Bhairab, the liar, so the feeling goes, will ultimately die vomiting blood. In fact, many of Bhairab's forms demand blood and are placated with animal sacrifices—especially on the Black Night of Dasain when thousands of animals die throughout the Valley, their blood spurting onto Bhairab images.

After pointing out the Kalo Bhairab to our guest and watching a fortune-teller plying his trade in front of the image, we walk south, soon coming to the main Durbar Square where business thrives amid throngs of people. Thirty yards southwest of here rises the Kasthamandap temple, a wooden Malla structure from which Kathmandu derives its name. (Kathmandu is a combination of two words: *kath* [wood] and *mandu* [temple]. One sometimes sees the word spelled Ka*t*mandu with a hard *t*, not the softer palatal *th*, but according to the origins of the word and the Nepali pronunciation, Ka*th*mandu is correct.) In any case, legend has it that this temple was built from the wood of one mighty mythological tree. While most authorities feel that the site dates from the founding of Kathmandu City in A.D. 723 (Kathmandu was then called Kantipur, "beautiful city"), the actual age of the structure is estimated at between three hundred and five hundred years old. The building, of rather simple design, stands three tiers high, with much of the superstructure weight resting on four massive wooden columns. And one can walk through its unusually open and airy lower floor to view street life on the far side.

After studying the Kasthamandap, we backtrack to the south edge of the square and enter a sturdy building through a low passage initially guarded on both sides by large stone lions. Eventually we straighten up in a small courtyard overlooked by massive and elaborately carved window frames. The Kumari, or Virgin Goddess, of Kathmandu lives here.

The Kathmandu Kumari is a young Newari girl selected from the Sakya (goldsmith) clan. While many stories circulate about how she came to be venerated, a popular version goes as follows. Once upon a time, the beautiful goddess Taleju, the protective deity of the royal family, was playing cards and dice with the Newari king. Beside himself with her beauty, the king tried to touch the goddess, whereupon she vanished from sight. But not wishing to leave the kingdom unprotected, the goddess indicated that she would return in the form of a virgin Newari girl who must be worshiped as if she were the goddess herself.

The Kumari selection committee consists of priests and religious fathers, among whom is the chief caretaker of the Taleju temple. Likely candidates must first measure up to the thirty-two prescribed "perfections," which include well-proportioned nails, long toes, hands and feet veined like a duck's, chest like a lion's, neck like a conch shell, small delicate tongue, a clear serious voice, eyelashes like a cow's, a lustrous complexion, stiff hair growing naturally to the right, a body shaped like a banyan tree, and twenty-one other conditions. Prospects who pass these tests are then shut away in a dark room where recently severed heads from animal sacrifices and frightening noises combine to shock the girls. The new Kumari is easily singled out as she is the only one that does not cry or object. Once discovered, the Kumari is ensconced in her residence and will remain there until she sheds blood from a cut or menstruation.

The Indra Jatra festival, an annual event in the life of a Kumari, falls in September–October, when for three days a gaily decorated chariot, with the Kumari sitting placidly aboard, is pulled and pushed through streets and narrow lanes by straining devotees. Two other chariots follow the main vehicle, each bearing a young boy, the pair of them acting as male escorts representing Ganesh and Bhairab. The king of Nepal attends on the first of these days, for the little girl, embodying the royal Taleju goddess, will bestow a *tika*—often grains of rice mixed with colored powders, symbolic in Hindu practice—on the forehead of the person who is to rule Nepal for the next year. The Kumari phenomenon is basically Tantric Buddhist, but here again we see—with the tika applied to the Hindu king—the unique intermingling of Hinduism and Buddhism so common in the Valley.

The young Kumari retires upon reaching puberty. Some authors report that ex-Kumaris do not marry but become prostitutes. This is not so. While it is true that it may be difficult to find a husband for her (for it is widely held that the unlucky man will die young), the most recently retired Kumari is happily married and her husband very much alive. Moreover, the government recently increased the Kumari's pension, providing much-needed financial security for the ex-goddess.

While all large Newari cities and towns have a Kumari (apparently there are eleven Kumaris in the Valley), the Kathmandu Kumari is regarded as the original and is the only one considered to represent the force of the mighty Taleju. There are no Newari Kumaris outside the Valley.

On our way out of the Durbar Square, we skirt a large white building with Grecian columns—a relic of Rana times—to meet our car. From here we ride east, easing onto New Road, a three-block shopping district. Its crowded stores sell jewelry, curios, electric supplies, photo equipment, household appliances, food, stationery and general merchandise. Some of the most sparklingly lit shops are nicknamed "Hong Kong" stores, for they display goods imported from there and beyond. These emporia are usually jammed with customers, many from south of the border. And on the right of the street grows a large pipal fig tree, a city landmark that shades several idols as well as newspaper sellers dealing in local and Indian editions.

Car parking on New Road is limited to the center of the thoroughfare, with policemen clearing vehicles during the 9:30 to 10:30 and 16:30 to 17:30 rush hours. With central parking rather tight, one's car door, if opened too quickly, could be ripped off by a passing vehicle, but with the danger so obvious, accidents rarely happen.

Another traffic hazard, often spoken of as charming and of a rather minor nature, sets Kathmandu apart from many other capital cities. Sacred cows and bulls freely roam the streets and occasionally repose on them. Inexplicably, though, they seldom pass their leisure hours lying on busy New Road. Some do amble along the sidewalks and sometimes rest there, but few select the direct line of traffic.

The cows of Kathmandu may seem lost, but each has a "home" where she is looked after and to which she usually returns at night. Bulls do not. The latter, once dedicated to a temple, are turned loose to fend for themselves; no one in particular owns them. They may be fed frequently, however, by people with a special interest in a particular bull.

Driving under the New Road arch, a monument festooned with lion heads and other memorabilia, we leave the shopping district and confront a wide, grassy expanse fringed with jacaranda, poplar and ginkgo trees. This is the Tundikhel, or parade ground, which functions as a much-needed breathing space for citizens who congregate here on Saturdays or fine evenings. The Tundikhel also serves as a center for numerous national events, some of which are reviewed by the king from a pavilion at the north end. Two metal-plated arches rise on the periphery of the Tundikhel. These date from the coronation of King Birendra in 1975.

At the Tundikhel we turn right, driving along its western edge and past the "foreign post office" (for parcels only) before stopping at a red traffic light on the corner by the "general post office" (for letters, second-class mail and book post). From the car we can see a slender white tower, reminiscent of a Muslim minaret, standing tall against the gray sky. This is Bhim Sen's Tower, whose white spire, visible from many points in the Valley, forms Kathmandu's most conspicuous landmark. Bhim Sen Thapa, an early prime minister, erected this tower in the 1830s, apparently in memory of a dead queen. Initially the tower had eleven sections, as can be seen in a pen-and-ink sketch done by Oldfield in April 1853. Today only nine remain, the upper parts having toppled during severe earthquakes in 1856 and 1934. As late as 1948, bugles blown from the tower summoned troops and alerted the populace, but today the monument stands as a reminder of Nepalese history and appears illuminated on festive occasions.

With the green light, we turn east, passing in fifty yards the marbled Martyrs' Arch, noting the bronze casts of the dead men resting in cubicles open on two sides, and the bust of King Tribhuvan, placed at a higher level, which completes the arrangement.

In another hundred yards we emerge onto a wide boulevard at the end of which stands a large white building placed well behind imposing gates. Singha Durbar was the grand residence of the Rana prime ministers. When the latter lost power, the building, rumored to have a thousand rooms, was automatically converted into the national secretariat. (For anyone trying desperately to find a particular government office before closing hours, "a thousand rooms" seemed more like half the truth.)

One day in late June 1973, the morning dawned clear—so clear, in fact, that an unusual column of smoke and flames could be seen for many miles. Singha Durbar was on fire! An old building with an inner structure mostly of wood, it went up like the driest of tinder, the flames fed by stacks upon stacks of government papers. Explosions reverberated through the Valley as soldiers with dynamite tried to blast a gap between the burning and the unburned. People wept. A cherished landmark of Kathmandu was being destroyed. And all of it did burn except the front portion that housed the grand reception hall and the famous room of distorting mirrors. Virtually all the government files went up in flames, with charred shreds of paper floating down on plowed fields five or six miles away. Here was a severe test for the new government of young King Birendra. What would happen? The ensuing events impressed all. Government offices quickly resurfaced in different buildings around town. A collection, voluntary and nationwide, spontaneously developed, netting several million rupees for a new building—or buildings. Architectural drawings were solicited, the winner's plans suggesting a design similar to what had burned but with modern, efficient interiors protected against fire. Even today no one knows how the great fire started—faulty wiring perhaps. But after the initial shock died down, some people were heard to say that few events have helped streamline the governmental machinery as much as this one fire—and they may well be right.

Heading north from Singha Durbar, we continue past the next set of traffic lights (the ten automatic sets in Kathmandu are switched on during busy rush-hour periods) and turn left. Soon, on the right, we find the Royal Nepal Academy, housed in a modern-looking building set back amid well-tended gardens. Cultural programs, dances, music, art exhibitions and poetry readings are sponsored here. The academy serves as the nerve center of the artistic world in Kathmandu, and election to it is a high honor much sought after by young artists of all persuasions.

At the next junction we turn right to enter Durbar Marg, a broad street flanked by low buildings housing airline offices, curio shops and travel agencies. The boulevard ends at the new Royal Palace, where the king and his family reside. A tall tower designed in quasi-Nepalese style dominates the palace buildings, while the whole complex is surrounded by gardens and protected by a high metal fence. One may visit and marvel at the ancient palace in downtown Kathmandu, but visitors' tours are not scheduled in this new, working palace.

Two minutes from the palace is our point of departure—the Hotel Malla. Our guest, slightly tired from the walking and from the many stimuli that have crowded in on her since we pushed into old Kathmandu, needs time for a rest. But she wants to hear more about the people of the Valley, so we have invited her for a farewell dinner at our house.

The People
An Asian Blend

Our guest arrives just before 7:00 P.M. "This is an old Nepali house," I explain as I lead her in. "You'll have to watch your head, some of the lintels are quite low." The doorways of modern houses measure over six feet high, but few Nepalese are that tall and earlier dwellings often had door clearances of little more than five feet. Our house has some doors more than six feet high and some less—one has to remember which ones are which or cultivate a perpetual stoop. The former seems preferable, but occasionally a memory lapse causes anguished thoughts and a familiar swelling on one's noble brow.

Over dinner I brief our guest on the great and exciting variety of people that live in the Valley. According to the 1971 census (issued by the Central Bureau of Statistics), 618,911 people reside in the three districts of Kathmandu Valley. Of these, 45.70 per cent speak Nepali as a mother tongue, 46.23 speak Newari, 6.45 Tamang, and the remaining 1.62 assorted other languages.

The Nepali speakers, or Parbatis, came to Nepal and Kathmandu from India—especially western India. A major influx occurred during periods of persecution by Muslim invaders in the thirteenth and fourteenth centuries, but Parbatis have undoubtedly been settled in the lower hills of Nepal since very ancient times. Parbatis are of Aryan stock that first migrated, apparently, to western India many centuries ago, displacing the original Dravidian settlers.

While Parbatis have had much influence in the Valley for hundreds of years (the early Lichhavis were probably caste Hindus from India), they achieved ascendancy with the rise of Prithvi Narayan Shah who, as already mentioned, conquered the Valley some two hundred years ago. The present king is thus a Parbati from the Kshatriya (warrior) caste. So are the Ranas. In fact, these two family lines are closely related, for King Birendra is a Shah with a Rana mother, while Queen Aishwarya is a Rana. Thus the families have intermingled throughout Nepal's recent history.

The Parbatis maintain strict Hindu standards, with the country run on a religious pattern; indeed, Nepal is the only Hindu kingdom functioning today. The national calendar—the lunar Bikram Sambat variety—schedules festivals, holidays and family events by celestial positions. (Nepal is already into the twenty-first century, since A.D. 1980 is 2037 B.S.) Nepal's months change with the moon, their names strange to our ears: Paush, Magh, Karthik. . . .

The word "auspicious" means much in Kathmandu. To turn out well, things must be auspicious (i.e. in astrologically good order). Certain days of the week are auspicious for starting a journey or arriving back home. One would not think, for example, of terminating a trip on Saturday or beginning one on Tuesday (these restrictions apply, of course, only to the very orthodox of the Valley). Certain numbers are bad—anything ending in "0," for instance. Thus when King Birendra assumed the throne after the death of his father, he had to delay the actual coronation for eighteen months as the year was 2030, and in the following year the king's own age was thirty.

Besides unifying the country, the Parbatis installed their language—Nepali—as the lingua franca of the nation, and one can travel the breadth of Nepal today and everywhere find people who speak Nepali in very passable form. This is obviously of great help in the development of the nation. Interestingly, though, some women do not speak Nepali—even in Kathmandu Valley. In many instances women do not travel as far as men, and are consequently less exposed to outside influences.

"Newar" is a term heard frequently during a visit to Kathmandu. Today there are well over 350,000 people for whom Newari is the mother tongue, and an estimated ninety per cent of them live in the Valley. The Newari culture is completely fascinating. The early history of the Newars is obscure, but their language, quite different from Nepali, relates to the Tibeto-Burman linguistic family and would suggest ethnic origins from that direction. Another theory, as yet unsupported, has the Newars coming from India. In any case, the Newars exhibit a genetic mixture probably produced by the unique location of Kathmandu Valley.

Today the majority of Newars adhere to Hinduism and observe a weak caste system, but Buddhist Newars have also developed social divisions, with priests at the top and sweepers at the bottom. How strictly caste is maintained—both in Hindu and Buddhist Newari families—depends largely on the feelings of each family itself, or separate individuals.

While dominating the arts and commerce in the Valley, Newars also rank among the great festival-lovers of Nepal. Vast amounts of money are spent on celebrations—especially on elaborate feasts associated with religious occasions. The events in the life cycle of a Newar are those honored, more or less, throughout the family of man. Birth calls for great rejoicing, with deliveries done, in traditional households, by the older women of the family. Following labor, the mother stays unclean for thirty days. During this period, especially in orthodox Jyapu (Newari farmers) communities, her body is oiled and she will sit from time to time in the sun, naked from the waist up. The oil, it is felt, helps secure the joints made loose during labor. Especially nourishing foods, including milk and meat, must be consumed during this thirty-day recuperative period; onions, turnips, potatoes and some spinaches, though, remain completely taboo for the interim.

Occasionally a child may be born on a very inauspicious day. In this case, the baby will be wrapped (depending on how orthodox the family is) in rags and "thrown away" (deposited) in a drain. Soon afterward a second party, with prior arrangement, recovers the child and claims "ownership" of the infant. The baby has thus started a second or new life, the evil of the first inauspicious beginning being canceled. Now the original mother will pay a small sum to secure the baby's return, thus further removing the newborn from evil designs. Similarly, if a boy is born into a family that already has several girls, the mother may organize the same ritual to ensure that no evil befalls her only son.

In some Newari houses, a ceremony called *chokyoune* is held twelve days after birth. This ensures good luck. Prayers are recited while the child is washed all over and its nails cut. Following chokyoune, the child may wear clothes; previously it was only swaddled.

The rice-feeding, *pasni*, ceremony comes next. This important event occurs when girls reach four months of age and boys from five to six months. Rice, often clasped in the mandibles of a bird (a shrike), when touched to the lips of a child amid the chanting of prayers, ensures ease of speech and wisdom in later life.

Puberty rites demand that a girl be isolated for twelve days after her first menstruation; and she must see neither the sun nor men. But at the conclusion of this quarantine, a large party is held. Similarly, much rejoicing—and feasting—accompanies the induction of a boy into manhood. To save expense several boys may be initiated together; a recent event focused on boys ranging in age from six to twelve years.

In most Newari families, girls can be married with *full* ceremonial pomp only once in a lifetime. Many Newari girls first marry between the ages of five and ten. Shocking? Certainly! But when one discovers that the girl marries the fruit of the bel tree, outrage ceases. The bel fruit stands as a symbol of permanence, and the girl will remain married to it for the rest of her life. Should a later human husband die, the girl does not become an outcaste widow, but in principle is free to remarry.

A Newari human marriage, man to woman, develops between the ages of eighteen and twenty-two, with the male usually slightly older than the female; this second marriage (for the girl) receives much attention but not quite the full pomp of event number one. Normally arranged by the parents, a Newari marriage adheres to caste lines, with horoscopes—of utmost importance—determining the suitability of the couple in pre-wedding drama. Only auspicious seasons are suitable for weddings, the dates predetermined by the stars; and in propitious weeks, marriage bands can be seen playing loudly—and somewhat discordantly—up and down Kathmandu's streets. Sometimes, though, the disposition of the stars is particularly bad. Thus for a nine-month stretch in 1976 marriage was unthinkable; predictably, however, the flurry of band activity on the days prior to the long ban seemed more frenzied than usual.

Following marriage, no chronological events, other than yearly anniversaries, are observed. Should someone reach the age of seventy-seven, however, a great parade may be held, in which the revered ancient is carried about town on a brocaded palanquin. This celebration starts punctually in the seventy-seventh year, in the seventh month, on the seventh day and at the seventh minute after birth.

The death of a father or mother entails numerous ceremonial duties for sons. White, the color of mourning, must be worn for twelve months and appears commonly on Kathmandu streets, though the less orthodox will wear any color except red. Salt and meat must be avoided for the first thirteen days after the death of a parent, and some children will not drink milk for an entire year following the demise of a mother.

Family ties remain strong among the Newars, who are a remarkably gregarious people. They also live close together, their multistory brick houses cheek by jowl, often sharing common walls; and even when they move away from the Valley, settling along remote trade routes, the Newars adhere to their tightly knit living patterns. In the Valley itself one can easily tell a Newari community from a Parbati or Tamang one, for the last two groups prefer to live in separate houses, with space about. And in closely developed communities, joint Newari families naturally prevail; the largest one in the Valley (in Bhaktapur) reputedly numbers over two hundred members. Recent land-reform legislation, though, has set a ceiling on how much land a family—joint or otherwise—may own and is fragmenting joint families fairly rapidly.

Besides dominating business in the Valley, Newars are the great craftsmen of this region, their artisans using metal, stone, wood and clay as their media. Since earliest times, Newars have utilized designs and techniques stemming both from inherent inspiration and from outside sources. The images of gods and goddesses often followed Indian models. The great Gupta period (4th–6th century A.D.) flourished in the plains below Nepal, and much has been written about this "golden age" of Indian art; but once Gupta stylizations had found their way to Kathmandu, they were modified by the unique Newari genius. Exquisite Nepali bronze pieces from this period rank among the finest in Asia.

One particular aspect of the Newari genius stands out against the Kathmandu skyline: architecture. The pagoda-style temple, so characteristic of the Valley, may have been the prototype for pagodas throughout eastern Asia, each country modifying the original Newari idea (see Bernier's *The Temples of Nepal*, p. 5). Arniko, the most famous of early Nepalese architects, was called to Kublai Khan's court in Peking where, in the late thirteenth century, he became the Imperial Minister for Building and Arts, and is best known for the White Dagoba in Peking's Central Park.

Along with a magnificent art history, the Newars also developed their own written language—one of the few groups to do so in Nepal. This script, of a rather flowing form, derives from Sanskrit and appears to be complicated. Spoken Newari echoes throughout Kathmandu today—business is often conducted in it—but the written form (in prose or poetry) is fully appreciated only by a compact group of Newari specialists.

While Parbatis and Newars dominate the Kathmandu Valley population, most other ethnic groups in Nepal are also represented. Such minorities often gravitate together in downtown, multistory buildings. Sherpas, for example, originally from the slopes of Everest, are a common sight in Asan Tol, and within the past decade they have migrated in considerable numbers to Kathmandu—mainly for economic reasons. Traditional herdsmen and traders, these people are now active in businesses in the capital, and many are involved in the booming trekking outfits. Virtually all trekking companies hire Sherpas as their field staff, while several are run by the Sherpas themselves. Trekking Sherpas return to their highland slopes for extended holidays, but are essentially based in Kathmandu.

After Parbatis and Newars, the Tamangs constitute the next

most common residential group in the Valley. Tamangs exhibit Mongoloid features and speak a Tibeto-Burman language, and they certainly appear to have come from the north and east. They abound at the edge of the Valley and on hills near the capital, most probably forced there by later and more aggressive invaders. The early Kiranti, thought to have been ascendant in Kathmandu over two thousand years ago, are identified as Rai and Limbu—groups now found in eastern Nepal. Could the Kiranti have been partly Tamang? If not, how did the Tamangs come to be between Newari Kathmandu and Kiranti eastern Nepal? We do not know. Some day archeological exploration may uncover the answers.

In any case, numerous Tamangs live nowadays in or near the Valley, farming and herding. While adhering to Hindu festivals and rituals, they still retain, at the core, many animistic practices; witch doctors, for example, are much respected and very useful citizens in Tamang communities.

In former times, the word Tamang was synonymous with "coolie." Until comparatively recently, all goods arrived in the Valley on men's backs (the first motorable road only pushed through to Kathmandu in 1953), and most of them were carried by Tamangs laboring up and down the approaches to the Valley. Hence the rather derogatory connotation of the name. Individuals who managed through education to escape their lowly status often changed their names to "Lama," which has respected religious overtones. The times are changing, however, as a Tamang—retaining the name Tamang—is completing a Ph.D. in wildlife management at an American university.

After dinner, we drop our guest off at the hotel and return the next morning to take her to the airport (sadly, most travel itineraries, we find, allow too short a time for guests to fully sample the richness of this intriguing region). The airport bustles with activity as midmorning international jets arrive. Among the tourist passengers hovering in the international departure section, many of whom are on escorted tours, traveling Nepalese are easily spotted, for scented garlands obscure their necks and bright red tikas adorn their foreheads, placed there to ensure travel safety.

The airport of today, with its 10,000-foot runway receiving two- and four-engine jets, is a far cry from the same scene in the early 1950s when Nepal opened itself to modernization. Then, lumbering DC-3s landed on a grass strip and taxied to a grass-thatch shack—the terminal. And the airport's name? Cow Field, or Gauchar—a rather apt description. Few places better symbolize the changes that have gripped Kathmandu over the past decades. The continued rapid growth of aviation in Nepal keeps Tribhuvan International Airport authorities at their drawing boards, but still the crowds overtake them.

We say good-bye to our guest and wave her jet into the sky, waiting as the plane disappears beyond the blue hills rimming the Valley. She had spent three days in Kathmandu. Adequate? Hardly. But then one could never really see everything or delve into all aspects of life in the Valley, no matter how long one stayed.

◁ 1. Buddha's all-seeing eyes (*preceding page*) gaze out from each gilded face of the tower that crowns Swayambhu Stupa, just west of Kathmandu City.

2–4. Part of the flag-hung Swayambhu compound (*opposite*) contains a twin-roofed pagoda dedicated to the health-giving goddess Ajima. Elaborate reliefs called *torana* (*right*) and prayer wheels (*below*) decorate its walls.

5. A horn-blowing lama celebrates the Buddhist New Year at Swayambhu.

6. Swayambhu hill has been venerated for over two thousand years.

7. Hanuman, the popular Monkey God (*left*), sits swathed in red near the main entrance to Kathmandu's ancient palace. The statue—eyes chastely blindfolded, for Hanuman faces some erotic carvings on a nearby temple—was placed here by a Malla king over three hundred years ago.

8. The view *below* is of Basantpur Square, as seen from high up in the ancient palace, with the leaf-shaped tongues of wind-bells hanging below the eaves. The sound of ringing bells is supposed to attract the attention of the gods.

9-12. The image of the Seto Bhairab (*top left*) is on public view in Kathmandu for only three days, during the autumn Indra Jatra festival; at the height of the festival, the crowd jostles for some of the consecrated beer that flows from a bamboo spout inserted in the Bhairab's mouth. Both the Bakadesh Bhairab (*top right*) and the Akash Bhairab (*above right*) are smothered in fresh garlands at the same festival. And the terrifying Kalo Bhairab (*above left*) is permanently draped with a carved garland of severed heads.

13. Wood carving in the Valley has a long and impressive history. *Below* is part of Kathmandu's ancient palace, facing the inner courtyard called Nassal Chowk.

14–15. Details from the ancient pal-▷ ace: a doorjamb, *right* (note the string of beadlike skulls); and a weathered Bhairab, measuring about four by four and a half inches. Both are over two hundred years old.

16. The gaudy facade of Annapurna temple looks out over Asan Tol, one of the most congested squares in old Kathmandu. The temple is typical of the pagoda style that originated in the Valley.

17. Rani Pokhari (Queen's Pond) in downtown Kathmandu contains a small temple (*below*) dedicated to Shiva.

18–20. The present king's▷ coronation in 1975 was marked by a formal procession (*opposite above*) from Nassal Chowk, where the kings of Nepal are traditionally crowned, to the new Royal Palace (*top right*) via the parade ground called Tundikhel (*right*).

21. The eastern skyline of old Kathmandu, with the tall Taleju pagoda on the far left.

22. Taleju is the protective deity of the Kathmandu kings, and her temple is one of the largest in the Valley. It is thought to have been built by King Mahendra Malla in 1549.

23-25. Street scenes in downtown Kathmandu: a candle merchant smoking a hooka (his white clothes are a sign that he is in mourning for a dead parent); a storekeeper sorting women's hair ties, bracelets and beads; and young wives on the steps of the Mahadev temple.

26. Strings of hot peppers drying outside the window of a private house.

27. The vegetable market in Kathmandu (*below*).

28. A khukri dealer (*above*) on a slow morning.

29. A local "snack bar" offering deep-fried *malpowa*, cooked over a wood fire.

30. A woolen shawl wards off the chill of an early winter morning at a sidewalk market in Kathmandu (*preceding page*).

31–32. Snug in its makeshift crib, a child dozes while its parents (*below*) attend to their fruit and vegetable stand. (Apples, incidentally, are a popular winter fruit in the Valley.)

33. Tibetan masks, carpets, *thanka* (religious wall hangings)—and even copies of a Japanese wood-block print—festoon the second-floor windows of a Kathmandu store.

34. These hanks of dyed wool will be used in the manufacture of Tibetan rugs.

35–38. Animal sacrifice is an integral part of the great autumn festival of Dasain. The flocks shown on the *preceding page* will soon join other animals—such as those milling around Hanuman's statue (*bottom*)—in a gory fate. Even cars (*below*) are ritually anointed with blood as an insurance against accidents. And to ensure good luck in the coming year, everyone should ride at least once on the giant swings erected during this festival (*right*).

39–41. The festival of Tihar falls two weeks after Dasain, and garland sellers do brisk business. On the third day of Tihar, cows and bulls are bathed, garlanded and fed; and lights are set out everywhere, inviting Lakshmi, the Goddess of Wealth, to well-scrubbed hearths.

42. A boy less than twelve years old is chosen to represent the god Ganesh (*left*)—one of two male escorts of Kathmandu's Virgin Goddess during the Indra Jatra festival.

43. Masked dancers add a vivid touch to the Indra Jatra festival.

44. Women line up *below* for a glimpse of the Kumari, or Virgin Goddess, at her residence in Kathmandu.

45. Teej, a women's festival held toward the end of the monsoon, symbolizes purification and the desire for a happy marriage and a long life. The woman on the *left* is selling powder and other religious accessories for this occasion.

46. A group of women during Teej, with ritual offerings on leaf plates.

47–48. Excitement shows in the faces of a crowd watching the swaying tower of the Seto (White) Machendranath chariot (*opposite*) in downtown Kathmandu. During this festival, the Machendranath image is given its annual holy bath, and is repainted and reclothed.

49. A bonfire is lit on Swayambhu hill at the end of the Buddhist year, symbolizing the burning away of the past year's evil.

50–60. A gallery (*from top left to right*) of faces seen in the Valley: a Newar woman; a Newar boy with a popsicle; a Newar girl; a well-to-do Rana bride; a Tamang; a middle-aged Newar; a *sadhu*, or holy man, of Indian origin; a Sherpa woman; two Tibetans; a Brahmin grandmother; and a Rai from eastern Nepal.

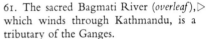

61. The sacred Bagmati River (*overleaf*), ▷ which winds through Kathmandu, is a tributary of the Ganges.

Patan
City of Art and Festivals

Take Patan, for example. We live in Patan. Years could be spent studying this locality alone. Patan, or Lalitpur (*lalit pur* means "city of art"), boasts the finest wood-carvers, the best bronze-casters, and possibly the most talented painters in the Valley.

Patan, one of four Valley city-states, is a tightly knit Newari city of some 59,000 people. Beyond the advent of electricity and some blacktopped streets, Patan has changed little over the centuries—in fairly striking contrast to Kathmandu itself, where travel agencies, hotels, restaurants and glossy shops crowd one upon the other. Patan has been left to its own devices—and its art.

Wood carving of the highest level of Asian craftsmanship has developed in Patan. While no wooden buildings can really be dated before A.D. 1400, carving has been a tradition here for at least a thousand years, and probably more. Excitingly, master carvers still exist, working with time-honored religious patterns handed down through the years, turning out new pieces as they sit beneath exquisite wooden relics of the past. Modern innovations do occur, but they form a minor part of current work. Small carved owls, for instance, sell to Western clients who favor such birds, but owls are hardly something a Newar would carve without economic incentive; these birds are considered evil omens. Monetary reward, however, has a way of overcoming

79

superstition. Newari carving reaches its zenith, however, in window frames and doorjambs.

The great bronzes of the Valley also originate in Patan. These pieces, cast in the lost-wax process, are images of gods and goddesses with numerous arms and sometimes multiple heads. The technique involves molding beeswax into the desired form and then covering the wax with a layer of fine clay and rice-chaff mixture. Meanwhile clay is also deftly tucked inside the image. Once the clay is heated, the wax melts out through a hole in the bottom to leave a hollow mold, hence the name "lost wax." When molten bronze has been poured inside and has cooled, the mold will be broken and the piece released for further refining before sale. The entire process from wax molding to filing takes about a week for a smallish piece.

Innovation, however, is not a key word among bronze masters; designs remain traditional. Many pieces, once finished, are chemically "aged"—a process that takes less than a full day—and some darkened items have been known to end up as "antiques" stuffed into the suitcases of tourists in furtive quest of bargains in ancient bronzes. All should carefully note that government regulations strictly forbid the export of *any authentic* antique (i.e. over a hundred years old) that was manufactured in Nepal. To clear questionable items through customs, one must have a seal from the Archeological Department certifying the object's lack of antiquity. So many fine objects of religious and archeological importance are spread about the Valley, and most of them poorly guarded, that it is little wonder that over the years part of this rich heritage has disappeared. Idol-lifting still occurs, although thankfully on a much reduced scale, with the thieves often apprehended by efficient police.

Patan, preeminently a city of art, does not lag behind other Newari communities in the quantity or spirit of its festivities. The

Red or Rato Machendranath, a special festival unique to Patan, lasts nearly a month and culminates in the showing of the Jewel Vest. This festival is an example of a local celebration attended by hundreds of people from different parts of the Valley.

The Red Machendranath has its origins, according to legend, in a Valley drought. Prayers for rain were to no avail, so the elders of Patan went searching far and wide for help. Finally they succeeded in attracting Machendra from his residence in Assam. Upon the god's arrival in Patan, the heavens opened, deluging the waiting fields and delivering the people of the Valley from disaster; and from that day on they have worshiped the god whose image is paraded through Patan in a grand vehicle. Machendra's chariot, a top-heavy affair, reaches nearly sixty feet into the sky, and its bamboo pinnacle is lovingly decorated with green boughs and glittering pendants. Should the chariot tip over and crash against someone's house, great good fortune supposedly befalls the occupants (thus the expenditure of a few rupees to repair the damage is of minor consequence). Power lines that interfere with this ancient occasion are cheerfully cut—allowing the teetering chariot to pass—and then restored in due course. Once the parade begins, each locality (tol) through which the chariot proceeds supplies manpower for locomotion, and tol families are also designated, on a rotational basis, to provide a large feast for local residents as the chariot passes.

The Jewel Vest shown on the final day of the festival has a story all to itself. It seems that Nagini, the wife of the great cobra god Nag (who dwells under Taudha Pond, near Chobar), fell sick. No amount of ministrations on the part of Nag had any effect, so he went in search of help, leaving his subterranean abode. Once aboveground, he chanced to meet a wise man traveling along the same road. On learning of Nagini's illness, the man accompanied Nag underground and, with good fortune, cured the serpent consort. Overjoyed, Nag presented the wise man with a jewel-studded vest, and, bidding them good-bye, the man started forth with the vest tucked under his robes. Soon he chanced to meet an evil spirit who at once detected and coveted the jewels. But the wise man, being what he was, perceived the evil designs of the demon and quickly gave the vest to the Machendranath temple, where it remains to this day.

The climax of the festival occurs when the great crowd catches a glimpse of the small dark garment as it is displayed from the four corners of the grand chariot. The king of Nepal also attends to pay homage to Machendra. In the auspicious wake of this event, rice can be planted, and as the Red Machendranath usually falls in May (just preceding the monsoon), it is well timed. Occasionally, though, the stars foretell disaster should observances be held at the usual season, so the matter must be delayed. In 1976, for instance, the festival was three months "late," finishing in mid-September. Nonetheless, rice was planted in June that year, under special dispensation—and did well.

While the Red Machendranath remains the biggest festival in Patan, the people here also celebrate with considerable vigor many other local holidays, as well as those common to the valley or the nation as a whole. The most important—and certainly the grandest in all Hindu Nepal—is Dasain. Dasain (or Dashera) is observed by Hindus as the period when the god Rama overcame Ravana, the evil King of the Demon Hordes. And although this very popular festival is based on the Ramayana epic, the event takes on ramifications in Nepal unique to this area.

Dasain lasts for two weeks, beginning with the new moon of Karthik (usually starting in about mid-October); and, during this period, offices are closed and many stores remain shuttered, so that little business (or repair work) can be done. Everyone joins in the holiday mood. The weather cooperates, too, as Dasain falls after the monsoon, when blue morning skies give way to afternoon cumulus clouds. Merrymaking continues for the entire fortnight, but four days are of special importance.

On Fulpati, the "Day of Flowers and Leaves," specially blessed plants are brought to Kathmandu from the town of Gurkha, the ancestral home of the Gurkha kings. After watching a spectacle staged on the Tundikhel by the royal army, the king then visits the Kathmandu Durbar for traditional ceremonies.

The following day, Asthami (actually the eighth day of Dasain), is marked by zealous fasting in preparation for the Black Night of Dasain, or Kalratri, when literally thousands of animals are slaughtered at shrines and temples in the Valley and, indeed, throughout Hindu Nepal, and images of the Goddess of Destruction and Bhairab, her male consort, are bathed in blood.

Sacrificing continues on the ninth day, Nawami, with many animals—buffaloes, goats, sheep, chickens, even doves (depending on what one can afford)—meeting their ends. All vehicles, from small rickshaws to RNAC Boeing jets, are daubed with sacrificial blood, since Bhairab is the divine force of locomotion and a sacrifice to him elicits his protection from accidents. Sure enough, the way taxi drivers career around following Dasain makes it tempting to believe that some strange protective force is at work.

Vijaya Dashami, the tenth day of Dasain, is considered the peak of the holiday period as it commemorates the killing of Ravana and stands as a time of victory, when good triumphs over evil. It is also the day of the tika. Tikas, traditionally a symbol of victory and power, are massive and red on Vijaya Dashami and often include kernels of rice taken from sacred vessels. Any tikas worn by men or large tikas adorning women are strictly religious and proclaim in a conspicuous way that the wearer has performed some religious duty, though nowadays many women wear small tikas as beauty spots.

Dasain, a festival of a very personal nature, creates a general air of cheerfulness (often aided by quantities of potent liquid). Women in colorful saris cluster in small groups; families with well-dressed children (new clothes are practically a must) parade from house to house or from house to shrine. A good deal of money changes hands on this occasion—to purchase sacrificial animals, to buy clothes, and to provide the required feasts. A Dasain bonus, often consisting of up to a month's pay, is customarily given to employees. Still, debts do accumulate, hopefully to be paid back gradually during the ensuing months.

But one cannot rest for long following Dasain, as the great festival of Tihar begins with the new moon of Paush, two weeks after Dasain. Tihar is actively celebrated in Patan and other cities of the Valley, as well as in all Hindu Nepal. It is also observed in India as Diwali, but, as with Dasain, the Nepalese version assumes a character of its own.

Tihar runs for five days. "Crow Day" starts events, with each successive day devoted to a special theme. Crows are regarded as harbingers of misfortune, so propitiating them is of obvious advantage, and dishes of rice and other food are set out for the birds. The orthodox will feed the crows every day; others just this once. Luckily, Tihar does not coincide with the crows' nesting season, for nothing will obliterate the most evil omen of all—that of seeing crows mating. A shopkeeper near Bhim Sen's Tower told us that his father died less than a month after the merchant chanced to see a pair of copulating crows.

The second day dawns as "Dogs' Day." These animals, extremely numerous in Kathmandu, stand guard at the gates of heaven and also serve as a mount for Bhairab (cats, conversely, are considered evil and few roam the alleys of the city). A dog receives special food on "Dogs' Day," and not infrequently a red tika is pressed on its forehead, while a garland of marigolds and other autumn flowers, tailored to canine proportions, is draped about its neck. Apart from their religious function, dogs fulfill another important role in the Valley, for the pariah type feeds on human excreta, thus performing a vital ecological function in towns lacking toilets or sewerage systems.

The third day of Tihar is dedicated to the worship of cows; these animals receive garlands and tikas, and sometimes the devout will decorate the animals' bodies with appropriate designs. In addition, the cows may be washed, and special food is provided for them. In Hindu annals, the cow has been sacred for centuries, and today it plays an essential role in village life, where dung is used for fuel (little forest firewood is left), milk for food, and butter (*gheu*) for cooking. In lowland Nepal, oxen pull plows and carts, but one sees very few working animals in Kathmandu because, we are told, the sacred beasts cannot be used within one mile of a temple. Given this restriction, there are few places in the Valley where one could squeeze in a working ox.

People also scrub their houses on the third day of Tihar, readying the premises for the visit of Lakshmi, the Goddess of Wealth, whose arrival at midnight climaxes the entire festival. Lights are crucial on Lakshmi Puja, and they pop up everywhere: butter lamps winking, candles sputtering, and electric lights blazing. The Nepal Electricity Corporation busies itself decorating its own premises with strings of colored bulbs, as well as supplying additional electricity using diesel generators to augment the existing hydroelectric supply. In many respects, Tihar lighting reminds one of Christmas decorations. Suitable illumination and clear directions are important, for Lakshmi comes only to houses where preparations have been adequate. If satisfied with arrangements, she then gives her attention to the family money box where cash, account books, and checkbooks lie exposed (the benefits of her visit to accrue during the next year).

One's own body is worshiped on the fourth day, or Mha Puja. This celebration recognizes that part of the divine entity exists in each person—as well as in every living creature. To propitiate Yama, the Lord of Death, on this occasion is thought to prolong one's own life and that of one's family members. Elaborate rituals conducted after dark by the mother of the household mark the end of the ancient (also Newari) old year.

Bhai Tika, or "Brothers' Day," provokes great rejoicing on the fifth day as sisters bestow tikas and garlands on their brothers amid much feasting. The significance of the event rests in the ancient tale of a girl whose brother lay sick. Yama approached the pair, but the girl pleaded eloquently with the god to delay death until she had finished worshiping her brother. The piety of the girl so entranced Yama that eventually he allowed the boy to remain alive. The tika on this day therefore signifies the hope that brothers so hallowed will be spared from death. Should no sister be present, a respected female friend or relative may be asked to do the honors.

The fifth day of Tihar is also the ancient New Year's Day, but this ranks as only one of several celebrated during the 365-day seasonal cycle in Kathmandu. In fact, the Valley observes the Newari New Year (October), the Western (January), Tibetan or Buddhist (January), Nepali (April) and Muslim (variable). The years attained in each calendar also differ, so that A.D. 1980 is equivalent to 1101 (Newari), 2037 (Nepali), the Year of the Elder Metal Monkey (Tibetan) and 1400 (Muslim). In most proceedings in the Valley, though, the Nepali system comes first and the Western second.

Gambling, frowned upon by the authorities except under casino regulations, is overlooked during the five days of Tihar. Small pockets of men crowd around gaming tables placed outdoors; passersby are enticed to try their luck at dice thrown on elaborately designed boards, often staffed by enterprising youths. High-stake gamblers usually remain behind closed doors. Thus the debts of Dasain can be—and often are—compounded on Tihar.

The list of Valley festivals seems endless. Harvest excitement follows Tihar, and then the god Rama weds Sita. In late winter, Shivratri draws large crowds to Pashupati. As spring sets in so does Holi, when red powder and colored water are thrown on willing passersby (the willing aspect decreed by government). Late spring brings the horse festival to the Tundikhel, and one moves on to the full moon of Chaitra, when the faithful bathe at the twenty-two waterspouts of Balaju. The Nepali New Year's Day occurs in April, and is followed by devotions for one's departed mother. In mid-monsoon, the defeat of the devils and their banishment to the underworld is remembered in the Ghantakarna festival. The monsoon also ushers in Gai Jatra parades when cows or cow effigies walk the streets, organized by people who have lost relatives during the preceding year (the cows push open the gates of heaven). The festival of the Snake God, Nag Panchami, arrives next, and thousands of printed or painted images of snakes appear plastered over doorways throughout the Valley. Late in the monsoon season, homage is paid to one's departed father at Gokarna, and much red is worn on Teej, a women's festival which, held as the monsoon wanes, brings us full circle to Indra Jatra, Dasain and Tihar.

Most Newars in the Valley celebrate many of the above as well as numerous other events of a family or national character. One wonders that they have time for such mundane things as work. Yet the Newars retain a reputation as first-class craftsmen and business people. Work hard and play hard seems to be their motto.

The work of the Newars is certainly evident in Patan, where the spacious, red-hued Durbar Square is even grander than that of Kathmandu. Detailed examples of Newari artistic genius embellish the buildings of the square, which include the ancient palace, complete with snake-decorated royal bathtub. Most of these buildings adhere to the typical Newari brick and pagoda-roof style, but conspicuous in its departure from the norm is a stone edifice with many pinnacles. This Krishna temple, fashioned after the Indian shikara style, dates from A.D. 1723. The temple has eight sides—a figure rumored to correspond to the number of wives who committed *sati* (jumping on the funeral pyre) when their Newari king died. Shikara temples adorn the main squares of the major Valley cities, but occur only rarely away from these royal environs.

Eight hundred yards southeast of the Patan Durbar Square, we reach a unique temple constructed entirely of brick. This Temple of a Thousand Buddhas, or Mahabauddha, has small carved Buddha images, floral designs, or other figures on each out-facing portion (of one or more bricks); and the style is again shikara, modeled on a temple in Bodhgaya, in India. The Patan temple dates from before A.D. 1585 (see Percival Landon's *Nepal*, p. 41), but apparently the top two-thirds needed rebuilding after the 1934 earthquake. The way the temple's surroundings seem to press in upon it only serves to accentuate the incredible number and infinite repetition of its carvings.

Shifting now slightly northwest of the Durbar Square, we duck through a narrow passage and emerge at the golden Mahavihara temple. This Buddhist structure, very ornately gilded and decorated, is surrounded by buildings with large prayer rooms formerly used by Buddhist lamas. In past times, Patan had many such monasteries, called *vihara*, woven into the structure of the city, but most have gradually been transformed into living quarters for local people, thus losing their monastic flavor.

Leaving the square and driving some two miles southwest, we approach a series of prayer flags and Buddhist prayer stones. A melodic chant fills the air, emanating from a long, shedlike building on the right. We are now at the Tibetan refugee center in Jawalakhel where the weavers are at work, skillfully and rapidly tying knots (between 70,000 and 140,000 per square yard) of pure wool to make their delightful rugs. Patterns follow traditional geometrical designs as well as floral and animal motifs; a happy yak with a flying tail, a dragon in red, yellow, and blue, and a Tibetan symbol for good fortune are popular. Refugees flooded into the Valley at the time of the Chinese take-over in Tibet; some settled here and others continued south to India. More and more Tibetans are now leaving the refugee center to enter business on their own and thus integrate into society.

One final diversion is to the Kathmandu Zoo, located not far from the Tibetan center. The zoo was founded in the 1930s by Prime Minister Juddha S.S.J.B. Rana, more or less as a private collection of animals, and by the early 1970s only three living reminders of the earliest days survived: the white cockatoo, the old rhinoceros and an aged keeper. By the mid-1970s only the cockatoo remained. With the exception of the fine bird section, where most species can fly a bit amid living vegetation, the main portion has not changed for many years. Plans are afoot to build a new zoo, one on modern lines with open-air enclosures, and one hopes these changes will proceed quickly to alleviate the cramped and uncomfortable aspects of the present setup. After all, the zoo provides an educational and entertaining outlet for the people, and over a thousand visitors usually click through the gates on Saturdays or other holidays.

Bhaktapur
and Other Ancient Sites

Over two hundred years ago, the conquering Gurkha king, Prithvi Narayan, united the Valley from what was then four separate city-states. We have already visited Kathmandu and Patan; now only Bhaktapur and Kirtipur remain to complete the survey.

Bhaktapur means the "city of devotees." Indeed, temples and shrines rise everywhere in this city (also called Bhadgaon), but hardly more so than in shrine-choked Patan or Kathmandu. If anything, though, Bhaktapur, located about eight miles east of Kathmandu City, has proved even less susceptible to change than Patan. It is an elongated city, built in the shape of a guitar. Fields fan out on all sides, while houses appear along a slight east–west ridge. The city, with a population of some forty thousand, has essentially one major street which passes through a large gate to reach the Durbar Square. As with Kathmandu and Patan, the Bhaktapur Newari king lived in his own stately palace, spending much of his time in a building with fifty-five ornate wooden windows. Nearby gleams the famous Golden Door, the brightest object in the square and a gateway to the Taleju temple—the royal temple of the Bhaktapur kings. The Taleju remains closed to non-Hindus, but Kodak, Fuji and Agfa do well enough by the Golden Door, whose scintillating, gilded Taleju goddess, Garuda (half man, half bird), and other deities, animals, floral designs and inscriptions attract even the most jaundiced eye. Protruding leogryphs with metal banners pendant from open mouths make the piece three-dimensional. This door, still in fine condition, is just over three hundred years old.

At the eastern end of Bhaktapur stands the Dattatraya temple, a moderately imposing structure which dates back to 1427, placing it among the oldest wooden buildings in the Valley. To the south of this comparatively open temple is a large, solid building, graced by some outstanding specimens of local woodwork. The much admired peacock window, a Newari masterpiece, is part of this structure, which at one time was a monastic complex but now houses the offices of a German-Nepali renovation and development team. The heavy and elaborate window frames here rival the work of the Patan master carvers.

As the sun sets behind the Chandragiri hills in the west and Kathmandu gradually falls into shadow, virtually the last rays to leave the Valley illuminate the tallest—and possibly the most impressive—temple in Nepal. The Naytapola temple of Taumadhi Tol stands five stories high, perched atop a raised platform, itself nine stages high; the total effect raises the temple over a hundred feet above the flagged courtyard. This unusual structure, thought to have been built in 1708, projects an aura of mystery, since it seems to have been dedicated to a secret Tantric goddess, and no image rests in the closed sanctuary. While the nearby Bhairab temple is well attended, with worshipers coming and going throughout the week, the Naytapola, largest of all Nepalese temples, stands aloof and unvisited except by curious tourists. Children play tag around the open porch, while others sit giggling on stone figures flanking the front steps. But no oil lamps flicker, no incense burns, and no bells ring inside; for the Naytapola is dedicated to the unseen.

The Naytapola is clearly no ordinary temple, and the stone

images guarding its front steps are themselves no ordinary statues. The first pair stand eight feet high and depict two famous wrestlers of Bhaktapur who had the strength of ten ordinary men. Following them in ascending order, each with ten times the strength of the figure immediately below, are elephants, lions, griffins and a pair of minor deities. And if one follows the implications of this visible hierarchy, the mysterious goddess reigning unseen inside would be ten times stronger than these minor deities and hence a million times stronger than mortal man.

Kirtipur, the fourth ancient city-state of the Valley, enjoys a commanding view, located as it is on a hill toward the western edge of the bowl and about two miles from Kathmandu City. For some reason, Kirtipur attained neither the artistic nor economic prominence of its three sister cities and was eventually absorbed into the administration of Patan. Even today, Kirtipur remains the most isolated and unchanged of all the Valley's towns; the ancient Kirtipur Durbar shown deteriorating in sketches done in the 1850s is still falling apart. The main temple of note, the Tiger Bhairab, is built on an uncommon rectangular pattern, instead of square, but the image of the tiger, often described as unusually fierce, remains hidden from view for non-Hindus. Given these circumstances, and if one feels at all squeamish about rudimentary sanitation, a visit to Kirtipur is not particularly recommended.

A stop at Pashupati, however, is mandatory. Here, crowding the flanks of the slow-moving Bagmati River, is the greatest concentration of Hindu temples and shrines in the Valley—comprising the grand Golden Temple of Pashupati itself. For Hindus, this area ranks as the most sacred in the Valley, indeed in all Nepal. The orthodox feel that to die here, toes immersed in the sacred waters of the Bagmati, frees them from the cycle of rebirth. The holiest sections remain closed to non-Hindus, but the Golden Temple, along with bathing scenes, cremations and other religious activities, may be observed from the opposite hill. Pashupati, sacred for many centuries, is probably one of the oldest occupied sites in the Valley. A large palace, no longer extant but described in early Chinese writings, may have stood here. But much archeological work remains to be done.

Finally, no visit to Kathmandu would be complete without a glimpse of Bodhnath or Baudha Stupa, a Tibetan Buddhist structure set a mile northeast of Pashupati. The white dome, splashed with saffron color-wash and larger than that at Swayambhu, occupies a setting more open than the latter. Curio shops ring the courtyard, and the residence of the Chini Lama, also equipped with saleable items, stands just north of the stupa. Baudha is a pilgrim center, attracting Buddhist devotees from the high Himalayan regions, and two monasteries function here, one located near the stupa and another a quarter of a mile to the north. Red-robed lamas, pilgrims from the north, and local people come to walk round and round the stupa, spinning the many prayer wheels as they go and chanting sacred mantras beneath colorful, flapping prayer flags.

◁62. Patan, just south of Kathmandu, is an open treasurehouse of sculpted art and architecture. On the *preceding page* is Patan's brick Temple of a Thousand Buddhas, or Mahabauddha.

63–64. Kites have tangled with the fine bronze figure of King Narendra Malla (*above*) that crowns a central stone pillar in Patan's Durbar Square. Part of the square (*right*) is occupied by an octagonal Krishna temple (on the far right of the scene).

65. A store selling handmade baskets, brooms and rope in Patan.

66. A Patan street scene.

67. A Patan child exploring a roadside faucet.

68. Scales are widely used in Patan, where even standard items such as brass jugs are sold by their weight, adding considerable time to transactions.

70. *Overleaf* is one of the curio shops▷ that have proliferated in Patan with the rise of the tourist industry.

69. The entrance to a small shrine inside the palace in Patan.

73. *Below* is Patan's own Virgin Goddess, seen in all her finery at the Red Machendranath festival.

71–72. A bronze streamer, or *pataka* (*above*), decorates the tower of the chariot (*below*) wheeled through Patan in the Rato (Red) Machendranath festival. This grand summer festival is held to commemorate the saving of the Valley from drought.

74. The climax of the festival is reached▷ on its final day, when the Jewel Vest (*opposite*) is held aloft.

76. The Golden Temple of Pashu-▷
pati (*opposite*) is the holiest Hindu
shrine in Nepal.

75. Rhesus macaque monkeys patrol the
neighborhood of Pashupati on the lookout for
food.

77. Bathing and cremation ghats flank the Bagmati River at Pashupati (*preceding page*). Special spiritual benefits are thought to derive from immersion here, particularly on auspicious days.

78. The five shrines of Panchamukhi Mahadev, at the southern edge of Pashupati, contain Shiva lingams. Ficus vegetation decorates, inadvertently, most of these comparatively modern buildings.

79. Rest houses (*above*) called *dharamshala* are common in the Pashupati area, catering to pilgrims from distant parts as well as local people.

80. Shankaracharya, a great Indian guru, sits in marble with attendant disciples. The group is now housed in a modern temple near the rear entrance of the main Pashupati temple.

81. The prayer flags this child is playing with will soon join others fluttering above the dome of Baudha Stupa.

82. Baudha (*opposite*) is a focus for ▷ Lamaistic Buddhism in Nepal, and one of the Buddha's bones is said to be enshrined in the stupa's gilded pinnacle.

83. The pellet of rice grains fixed in red paste and placed on this stone head indicates that the deity, located near the Bhaktapur Durbar Square, has recently been worshiped.

84. The steps leading up to the towering Naytapola temple in Bhaktapur are flanked by pairs of stone wrestlers, elephants, lions, griffins and minor deities—each ten times stronger than the pair below it. Now virtually deserted, this early eighteenth-century structure is said to have been dedicated to a secret Tantric goddess.

85. The Golden Door of Bhaktapur is over three hundred years old. The section *above* focuses on the goddess Taleju, one of whose ten hands grasps the hair of a captive demon.

86. Kite-flying from the rooftops▷ of Bhaktapur (*overleaf*).

87. Various crafts thrive in Kathmandu Valley. At *right* is a Patan wood-carver working a piece of sal into the image of a deity.

88. A mask-maker from Thimi.

89. A silversmith polishing his work.

90. Tibetan refugees at their looms in Jawalakhel. Most of the wool used is from local Nepalese sheep, but the dyes are imported from India.

91. A girl employed in the growing textile industry.

92. The food-storage pots *below* are drying in the sun before being fired in open-air mounds covered with rice straw and sand. Glazing is not a tradition in the Valley.

Godaveri
Green Fields and Green Oaks

While wandering in the main cities of the Valley, one tends to forget that most of this region is under cultivation. A drive to Godaveri at the southeastern edge of the Valley, however, offers an excellent insight into the rural scene.

Leaving Patan, one comes immediately to open fields (at one time, the juxtaposition of houses and fields was perhaps the most charming aspect of suburban Kathmandu, but a great building boom has chewed up most of this attraction). Fields in the Valley are tilled entirely by human labor, the plowing, sowing, weeding and harvesting—incredible as it may seem—all done by hand. Hundreds of industrious Jyapus (the Newari farmers) work their land, raising fine crops in the fertile soil.

The Jyapu farming style involves men turning over foot-square clods of earth in neat lines, using short-handled hoes that require a deeply bent back with each thrust (young men usually take on this job). Then women, often robed in blouses and black skirts with red borders, move down the line, breaking the clods with long-handled wooden mallets. The fields now stand ready for sowing. Men sprinkle the seed; women cover it with earth.

Rice, the main crop of the Valley, can be planted only during the summer. The initial seedlings are massed together in tight bunches glowing light green on the land. When the appropriate time comes, they are transplanted by lines of gaily dressed women who, bent low over the young plants, deftly place them the required six inches apart. A festive air prevails. Love songs—usually composed on the spot—are often sung. These frequently become slightly risqué, for the songs are duets, the first part sung by a boy (or girl) and the answer, awaited by fellow planters, composed by the opposite sex. Much laughing and giggling accompanies these songs, and gaiety permeates the whole process of planting rice.

Nowadays, wheat flourishes as a major winter crop, but wheat-planting generates neither the songs nor the color of the rice season. Nonetheless, the Valley wears a golden cape twice a year (October for rice and May for wheat), with intervening patches of green vegetables and brilliant yellow mustard (grown for its oil). Vegetables do well in Kathmandu, growing to enormous sizes, with cauliflowers measuring three feet across (including the leaves), radishes two feet long, and turnips three.

Continuing along the Godaveri road, we soon pass some low-slung buildings surrounded by experimental plots: these are all part of the Kumaltar Experimental Farm. The government places great emphasis on agriculture, trying to improve all aspects of both plant-raising and animal husbandry by introducing farmers to new ideas. A recent seminar on beekeeping, for example, was attended by a designated number of farmers, some of whom had never really seen a bee. The participants collected a handsome daily fee for this four-day course, and hopefully this commendable government program will pay off in better honey production and more income at the village level.

The tall transmitting tower of Radio Nepal occupies a plot just beyond Kumaltar. Radio Nepal, a major unifying force in the country, beams music and talk programs across the land. But though music leads the popularity charts, affable Krishak Kaka

(Uncle Farmer), discussing agricultural problems, ranks a close second.

Swinging past the radio tower and down a little hill, we come to an open series of terraces flanking the road. These fields contribute to an unusual double crop: rice in the summer and bricks in winter. Brick-making from the local clay of the fields is an important business in the Valley. Since stones are not readily found in the alluvial soil here and all available trees have long since been felled, Kathmandu's buildings are of brick, and the same material has been used since earliest times.

Local brick-making involves scooping the soil from a field and pressing it into a mold that releases a rectangular-shaped chunk when turned upside down. These blocks are either sun-dried (not so common) or fired in large, squarish kilns that belch offensive smoke during the spring and winter months. (Pity the man who resides downwind from an active brick kiln!)

Brick-making can be turned into a profitable concern, and just ahead of us—on the left—stands a brick and tile factory, a modern plant that churns out great quantities of these building materials of a standard and price higher than the field variety. With great foresight, the Kathmandu city fathers recently passed an ordinance allowing only buildings with brick faces to be built within the city limits—a fine regulation when one sees the number of drab concrete boxes erected before the ban. One can only hope that other Valley towns will follow Kathmandu's lead, and there are indications that Patan is considering suitable measures.

The town of Harisiddhi, small and tile-roofed, dominates a hill beyond the brick factory. Compactly built in true Newari fashion (and almost completely rebuilt after the 1934 earthquake), its houses seem stitched to one another in long lines. Many such settlements (essentially farming communities) dot the 204 square miles of the Valley floor, each with people living in the center and fields radiating from this core. The centuries have produced little change in Harisiddhi; visiting it drops one back into the Middle Ages or beyond. One thing only sets this town apart from others of its kind—the presence of an unusual sect of priests, their white robes resembling skirts and their long hair tied in buns. The priests are said to be well versed in ancient Tantric practices.

Ascending toward Godaveri, one approaches the edge of the Valley and suddenly the housing changes from compact villages to independent dwellings, each separated from the other by hedges and gardens. The latter are Parbati houses, the walls daubed with red clay dug from nearby soil, and the roofs covered with tiles or thatch. Parbati villages are spread along the periphery of the Valley, where the residents grow rice in well-watered fields or corn in upland terraces.

Godaveri itself, at the base of forested hills, is one of the most delightful places within easy reach of Kathmandu. Former prime ministers constructed summer cottages here, though these buildings have now been taken over by a Jesuit boys school, and children's laughter echoes among the campus trees.

A marble quarry operates immediately west of the school, producing slabs for buildings and chips for terrazzo finishes. This ancient metamorphic rock, over three hundred million years old, comes complete with crinoid fossils. Most Himalayan foothill rocks are sedimentary, with pockets of metamorphics that include marble. Igneous formations usually occur at high elevations in the main Himalayan range, although some granite and schist do surface at the northern edge of the Valley.

But Godaveri is best known for its Royal Botanical Garden, attractively laid out with imported exotics and local plant varieties. The fern and orchid houses are particularly popular, as is the Japanese garden, wedged into the northwestern part of the scheme. Picnic parties gather here, especially on Saturdays when large groups of school and college students appear for cookouts. Rice and steaming curry are prepared just outside the garden fence and served on plates constructed of large leaves stitched together. Picnics, often closely associated with festivals, are a long-standing tradition in Nepal and have been part of the social fabric for centuries. At large picnics, participants usually sit cross-legged in a single line that bends to form the outline of a square, helpers moving down the front of the line, heaping food on plates. Service is quick and easy in this way—and the leaf plates are biodegradable.

For the naturalist or outdoor enthusiast, Godaveri is one of the most exciting and accessible places in the central Himalayan foothills, for it harbors a rich variety of plants and animals. Take butterflies, for instance. In April and May, butterflies—many of them gleaming swallowtails—flock to an array of scented flowers, while forest insects flit along shaded mountain streams. In fact, Godaveri is one of the best butterfly areas in the entire Himalayan system: over a hundred species, ranging from drab beaks to magnificent blue peacocks and rose windmills, have been seen here in one day. The scarce siren, known in only three places in the world, has been collected at Godaveri.

Similarly, Godaveri enjoys a wealth of bird fauna, greatly contributing to the total number of species found in the Valley (over four hundred). Berry-eating white-cheeked bulbuls attend low bushes while the orange-bellied chloropsis feeds among treetops. Brilliant barbets and somber laughing-thrushes call loudly from foliaged retreats as red-faced kalij pheasants scratch at leaf mulch in less disturbed areas. As with butterflies, it is possible to see over a hundred species of birds at Godaveri in a day—providing one is patient and reasonably familiar with those found in the subtropical Himalayas.

In a broad sense, the Godaveri area includes the forested hill of Phulchowki that rises above the inhabited sections. This lush region is the home of many plants, including four varieties of oak trees, their leaves remaining green even through frost-filled winter nights. In addition, dark chestnuts, wild walnuts, red rhododendrons and Himalayan maples are but a few of the species contained in this natural garden. Fittingly, orchids (Coelogynes, Dendrobiums and Cymbidiums) find Phulchowki favorable, for *phul chowki* means the "place of flowers." Here, in a subtropical or warm temperate climate, 529 species of plants (as listed by a government publication) are to be found, including pink morning glories, yellow corydalis, purple strobilanthes and a fine red polygonum.

Nagarjun, another good forest area but not quite as rich as Godaveri, lies at the northwestern edge of the Valley. This hill, extensively forested on its northern slopes and near the 6,430-foot summit, can be reached in about fifteen minutes by car from downtown Kathmandu, and assorted subtropical trees as well as numerous birds and butterflies are an attraction here. On recent occasions several visitors have even seen leopards and deer on the forested back slopes.

For many years, though, encroaching woodcutters nibbled month by month at Nagarjun's forest, changing dense vegetation to open scrub. But no longer. An imposing wall now guards Nagarjun, and entrance is restricted to those holding tickets. Furthermore, a twenty-one-mile road ringing the entire hill allows one to drive through this area, possibly stopping en route for a picnic lunch at the summit shrine. Thus Nagarjun, impressive by any standards, now remains fully protected by excellent government foresight. Few capital cities can boast of an outstanding forest containing wild leopards only fifteen minutes from the doors of smart new shopping emporia.

But among all the hills and dense forests that rim the Valley,

Phulchowki is still the major attraction. Emerging from the oak trees at Phulchowki's summit (at 9,100 feet elevation), we find not only the traditional shrine but also a fine new building with a large, metal-framed microwave tower. Far below, glimmering in the northwest, lies Kathmandu City, and beyond, stretched against the blue northern sky, a vast panorama of snow peaks extends for some two hundred miles, sweeping through a 180-degree arc from Annapurna to beyond Everest. A view from Phulchowki on a cloudless day is indeed one of the finest visual treats in the Himalayas.

The Developing Valley

The Phulchowki tower, surrounded by prickly leaved oak trees, symbolizes the new, emergent Nepal. No longer is the country shielded behind blue mountains, no longer stagnant, her people unconscious of an outside world that called Nepal mysterious. Nepal has taken her international place, and Kathmandu, her capital, leads the way.

Progress is evident everywhere in the Valley: the sound of jet engines in the air, blacktopped roads supporting bulging buses and heavy electric power lines, their towers etched silver against the ripening rice, all speak of change.

And rapid change there has been. Twenty years ago the fields below Kirtipur, for example, were familiar only to tradition-bound farmers and egrets. Some terraces are still visited by these snowy-white birds, but most have been absorbed by the educational facilities of Tribhuvan University: the library, the convocation hall, the physics building and many others.

The university, incorporated in 1959, is a new phenomenon (previously colleges existed, but no university), and it has been organized into a series of institutes: the institute of medicine, of Nepal and Asian studies, of science, of education and so on. Each institute has a dean and appropriate administrative officers. The university year is divided into semesters, with students subjected to periodic examinations as well as their year-end finals.

Besides keeping the student openings low (thus avoiding an increasingly severe graduate unemployment problem), the new university system requires that each graduate-degree candidate (master's or Ph.D. level) must spend nine months working in a village situation. This National Development Service Plan puts young people in touch with the realities that are Nepal. Similarly, through a "Back-to-the-Village" national campaign, government officials must spend some time each year in selected villages to maintain a sensitivity to rural needs.

In all aspects of development, we must remember that Nepal only embarked on this course in the early fifties. No long-standing traditions favor change or innovation. Before 1950 Nepal had little industry, rudimentary communications and an economy based on subsistence farming. Today Nepal has made significant strides in basics—not in numerous highrise condominiums, but in vital aspects such as improved education, better health care, finer agricultural strains and more efficient communications.

Capital is not being channeled into gaudy showpieces meant to impress. Instead it is earmarked for programs such as the primary-school textbook development scheme and the beekeeping seminar previously mentioned. And resources are being utilized in a planned way, with the prestigious National Planning Commission setting priorities and continually reviewing the progress of projects initiated under their supervision. CEDA, the Center for Economic Development and Administration, housed at the university, serves as both a seedbed for project ideas and a valuable training ground for administrators.

Aid missions are a common sight in Kathmandu. Much assistance is needed from outside, and many countries are willing to help Nepal. But more and more Nepalese are realizing that projects need to be examined carefully in order to eliminate the excesses and mistakes of the past. Aid can be well-meaning yet contribute little to what Nepal so vitally needs: the laying of a secure base for a strong nation of the future.

Thus Kathmandu Valley has changed, and will change further. The capital of a modern country cannot afford to be a living museum displaying merely a collection of Newari brick houses and pagodas built on patterns laid down a thousand years ago. And some of the "charm"—the differentness—of Kathmandu will disappear. This is inevitable. But authorities appreciate the significance of their unique Valley. Sections of unsurpassed beauty, particularly the Durbar Squares of the main cities, have already been set aside for preservation. Additional plans call for barring all further heavy industry from the Valley, a splendid move when one sees the effects of the smoke-belching cement factory at Chobar. Similarly, an electric trolley-bus line from Bhaktapur to Kathmandu will help reduce pollution from automotive exhaust. Also, wild areas such as Nagarjun have been saved, preserving a valuable reservoir of unique Himalayan plants and animals. Things must change. But Kathmandu, a former lake that shimmered below snow peaks, will remain, with careful planning, a rare jewel lodged in the blue foothills of the great Himalayas.

◁93. The bird's-eye view on the *preceding page* shows a rural village laid out in the open, non-Newari style.

94–96. Where wood is unavailable and kerosine and electricity are too expensive, cow-dung patties may be used as cooking fuel (*below*); and water will be drawn from wells (*right*). At the farmhouse *opposite*, grain has been laid out to dry.

97. Farmers taking a lunch break during the rice-planting season.

98. Winnowing rice beside the road to Thankot, at the western edge of the Valley.

99. Women threshing rice (*above*), photographed on the way to Godaveri. Fluted Peak (20,986 ft.) floats high in the background.

100. Rice terraces seen in ▷ September (*right*), on the northern rim of the Valley. The rice harvest is in October–November.

101–111. A miscellany of the Valley's flora and fauna (*from top left to right*): a robin dayal; a red lacewing; one of the jungle cats still seen occasionally on the outskirts of the Valley; a hanging bell-flower; cosmos; a yellow-cheeked tit-mouse; a day moth; a great horned owl; Gleichenia and Abacopteris ferns; Den-drobium orchids; and a common myna, which often nests in the walls of Kath-mandu houses.

112. Cattle egrets feed among grazing sheep and goats on the banks of the Bagmati River.

THIS BEAUTIFUL WORLD